Reinvent Your Kitchen

By Christine E. Barnes and the Editors of Sunset Books

MENLO PARK · CALIFORNIA

SUNSET BOOKS

VICE PRESIDENT, GENERAL MANAGER: Richard A. Smeby

VICE PRESIDENT, EDITORIAL DIRECTOR: Bob Doyle

PRODUCTION DIRECTOR: Lory Day

DIRECTOR OPERATIONS: Rosann Sutherland

ART DIRECTOR: Vasken Guiragossian

STAFF FOR THIS BOOK

DEVELOPMENTAL EDITOR: Linda J. Selden

PROJECT DESIGNERS: Melinda D. Douros, Heidi M. Emmett,
D. Kimberly Smith, and Debra S. Weiss

COPY EDITOR AND INDEXER: Julie Harris

PHOTO DIRECTOR/STYLIST: JoAnn Masaoka Van Atta

DESIGN: Dorothy Marschall/Marschall Design

PAGE PRODUCTION: Maureen Spuhler

ILLUSTRATOR: Beverley Bozarth Colgan

PRINCIPAL PHOTOGRAPHER: E. Andrew McKinney

PREPRESS COORDINATOR: Danielle Javier

PROOFREADER: Mary Roybal

10 9 8 7 6 5 4 3 2 1

ISBN 0-376-01792-9
Library of Congress Control Number: 2002100917
Printed in the United States of America

For additional copies of *Reinvent Your Kitchen* or any other
Sunset book, call 1-800-526-5111 or see our web site at
www.sunsetbooks.com

COVER: The reinvention of this open kitchen offers a visual
feast of gleaming granite tile, frescoed walls, and an island
wallpapered and waxed to look like worn leather.
INTERIOR DESIGN: Heidi M. Emmett
PHOTOGRAPHY: E. Andrew McKinney
COVER DESIGN: Vasken Guiragossian
PHOTO DIRECTION: JoAnn Masaoka Van Atta

DESIGN CREDITS

Christine E. Barnes: 86, 108,
118, 124, 125, 126, 127

Melinda D. Douros: 95, 130,
134, 138, 142, 143, 144

Heidi M. Emmett: 10, 50, 51,
54, 56, 58, 73, 76, 78, 79, 80, 81,
82, 83, 108, 113, 118

Dale Miller: 10, 14, 16, 20, 21

**D. Kimberly Smith/Deer
Creek Design:** 24, 26, 66, 88,
95, 130, 134, 138, 142, 143, 144

Debra S. Weiss: 14, 16, 32, 44,
50, 54, 70, 81, 82, 108, 118,
125, 126, 127

**Karen Austin, CKD/Creative
Kitchens & Baths:** 22, 49

H & J Custom Woodworking:
138

**Kim Olson/K. D. Olson
Construction:** 134

Rich Ramey: 92

Woodgrain Woodworks: 36,
49, 102, 127

Somewhere between redecorating and remodeling is the reality most of us face when we decide to change the look of our homes. Out of necessity, we adapt what we have, incorporating new furnishings and features as our budgets allow. Fortunately, working with what you have does not mean settling for less than what you want. Success is as much about attitude as it is about such tangibles as paint, tile, and fabric. Think of it as the "reinvent spirit."

This spirit calls for a sense of adventure, a willingness to consider every element in your room as you formulate your plan. Three of the kitchens on the following pages are total decorating packages—new wall color, counters, cabinet doors, and floors, along with the finishing touches. Although the effects are dramatic, these major changes are easy to achieve because the steps are simple and the supplies are readily available. The remaining kitchens present doable projects and quick decorating ideas that build on the good "bones" of each room.

Last—but far from least—reinvention includes the satisfaction that comes from personal effort. Work hard, but be sure to enjoy the process and take pride in what you create. That's the reinvent spirit.

Behind every successful room featured in this book is a team of talented and generous people. We would like to thank the following individuals and businesses for their assistance: Karen Austin/Creative Kitchens & Baths, Broad Street Furnishings, Dovetail Design, Dunn-Edwards Paints, enVisions, K. D. Olson Construction, Andrew J. Sellery, Sierra Tile & Stone, Sarah Weiss, Woodgrain Woodworks, and Young's Carpet One. A special thanks to the homeowners who invited us into their homes: Cindy and Guy Greever, Dale and Gary Miller, and Debbie and Rich Ramey.

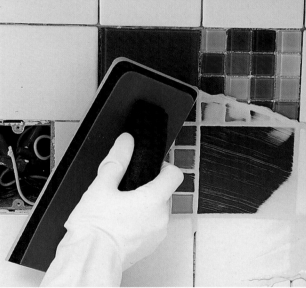

The Heart of the Home

It's the hub of activity, the place in your house where everyone seems to end up. No wonder the kitchen is the most redone room in the home. We *live* in our kitchens, so we want them to be rooms we enjoy. ∾ The kitchen is ripe for reinvention for another reason: remodeling a kitchen is more expensive than just about any other home improvement project.

Cottage Style features a mix of vintage textiles

Wouldn't it be great to work with what you have and add new features to create a fresh look—without a major investment? ∾ That's just what happened in the six kitchens you will see on the following pages. There were no true remodeling projects, and the budgets were modest by kitchen standards, but the transforma-

Natural Charm exudes from a cozy kitchen with a leafy theme

tions were dramatic just the same. You'll find a variety of styles, including charming cottage, updated country, breezy coastal, and lively retro. There's even a kitchen that makes use of materials more typically found in an industrial setting. ∾ Woodworking projects include a freestanding pantry, microwave

Surface Appeal comes from a blend of actual and visual textures

cabinet, and cutting-board

cart. Other projects show you how to "antique" an existing hutch, add wood legs to an island, tile a backsplash, and cover the sides of stock cabinets with beadboard.

Valances, pillows, and floorcloths add color and pattern and soften kitchen settings. Although these kitchens feature distinctive looks, many of the projects are interchangeable, allowing you to combine elements from different Marine colors and materials make for a dramatic Sea Change rooms for an original decorating plan. ᔕ A number of features in this book

help make the projects easy to pursue with confidence. A colored tab at the start of each project tells you the approximate time commitment, such as "Do It Today" and "In a Weekend," or identify it as a special type of project, such as Fresh, lively colors and patterns are Retro Active "Wood Shop" or "Sewing Workshop." Simple instructions, photographs, and illustra-

tions guide you through the step-by-step process; tips sprinkled throughout keep you on track. In the "Fresh Ideas" sections, you'll see the finishing touches that make each kitchen special. ᔕ Ready to reinvent your kitchen? Turn the page. Concrete, metal, and wood display Industrial Class

Cottage Style

THIS TINY KITCHEN AND COZY EATING AREA already possessed cottage charm—what they begged for was a dose of primary color and a mix of cheery prints to bring out their character. The home-owner's collection of kitchen textiles from the 1940s and 1950s provided both the color scheme and the pattern interest. Vibrant red paint, matched to the floorcloth, energizes the kitchen walls and defines the space; a richer yellow in the dining area holds its own against the red. The fabrics in the floorcloth, window treatments, and chair cushions pull it all together in vintage style.

Warm pine cabinets, handsome wood floors, and crisp white appliances were a real decorating plus in this small space, but their impact was limited by the pale walls.

MATERIALS

Fabric for face
of valance*

Fabric for lining*

Fabric scissors

Flexible tape measure

Thread to blend

Pins

Glass buttons

White latex paint

Gloves

Paintbrush

Wrought-iron rod

Clean rag

Glass doorknobs fitted
as finials

Curtain-rod brackets

*See Steps 1 and 2
for yardage.*

SEWING WORKSHOP

Button Valance

ELEGANT GLASS BUTTONS and a casual striped cotton fabric combine in this lighthearted tab-top window treatment, designed to harmonize with the flea-market chandelier and to match a sofa in the living room. Real buttonholes make taking the valance off for dry cleaning easy. Vintage glass doorknobs, fitted for duty as finials, screw onto the ends of wrought-iron curtain rods. (For how-to information, see the tip on the facing page.)

FINISHED SIZE

12 inches long
(not including tabs)
by 78 inches

Determining the Yardage

1 Measure the width of your window and multiply by 1¼ for gentle fullness. Divide that number by the width of your fabric (most home decorating fabric measures 54 inches wide) and round up to the nearest whole number to get the number of pieces you'll need to cut. Then, multiply the number of pieces by 16 inches (you'll be cutting the valance to 13½ inches long; the additional inches allow for error). Divide by 36 inches for the yards needed. Add extra inches for the tabs; see Step 5 to determine the number and size of the tabs.

2 Calculate yardage for the lining in the same manner, but do not add extra for tabs.

Preparing the Pieces

3 From the face fabric, cut the required number of pieces (deter-mined in Step 1) 13½ inches long by the width of your fabric. Trim off the selvages. With right sides together, join the trimmed edges, using a ¼-inch seam allowance, to make one strip; press the seam allowances open. Trim the strip to 1¼ times the width of your window.

4 Cut the lining pieces 11½ inch-es long; trim, join, and press as you did the face fabric.

5 Determine the tab width, length, spacing, and number as follows:

Tab width depends on the size of the buttons. (These tabs were cut 2¼ inches wide.)

To determine tab length, loop a flexible tape measure around your rod and pinch the tape together at the desired distance below the rod. The length of the loop is the finished length of the tabs. Add ½ inch for two ¼-inch seam allowances. (These tabs were cut 8 inches long.)

Tab spacing may depend on the fabric's design; with a striped fabric such as this one, match the tabs to the stripes. (The spacing between these tabs is 10 inches.) The spac-ing will determine the number of tabs.

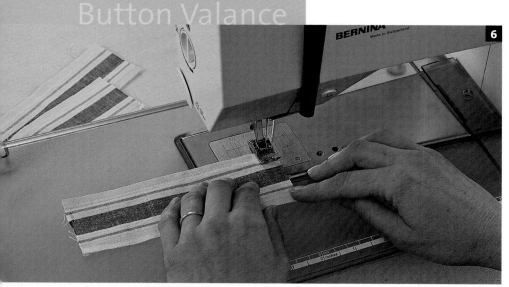

Making the Valance

6 For each tab, cut two pieces of face fabric to the measurements you determined in Step 5. With right sides together and raw edges aligned, pin and stitch the pieces on the lengthwise edges using a ¼-inch seam allowance. Stitch across one end using the same seam allowance. Turn the tab right side out and press.

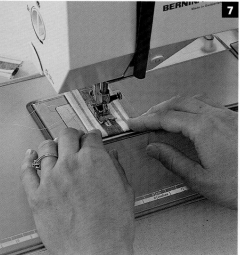

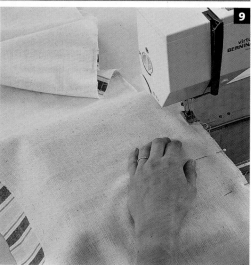

7 Make a buttonhole near the hemmed edge of each tab. (The side you are working on will be the right side of the tab.)

8 With the buttonholes right side up, pin the tabs' raw edges to the raw edges of the face fabric, placing the first and last tabs 1 inch from the ends; baste.

9 Right sides together and raw edges aligned, pin the lining to the upper edge of the face fabric, encasing the tabs. Stitch, using a ¼-inch seam allowance. (The other edge of the lining will be shorter than the face fabric.)

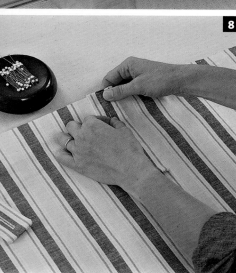

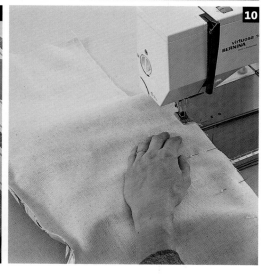

10 With right sides still together, bring the remaining raw edge of the lining to the remaining raw edge of the face fabric, forming a tube. Pin and stitch the lining and face fabric on the hem edge, using a ¼-inch seam allowance.

11 Turn the valance right side out and press the upper edge and the hem edge. Turn in the raw edges at each end ½ inch; press and pin.

12 Blindstitch each end of the valance.

13 Carefully cut the buttonholes. Sew each button to the top of the valance, just below each tab. Button the tabs.

Painting the Curtain Rod

14 Mix white latex paint and water to the consistency of cream; brush it onto the rod.

15 Rub off some of the paint with a rag to reveal the rod's original color. Let dry.

Installing the Valance

16 Feed the valance onto the rod; screw on the finials. Rest the rod and valance in the curtain-rod brackets. Have two helpers hold the treatment above the window to determine bracket placement. (On a sliding glass door, position the valance so its lower edge just covers the top of the door.) Install the brackets, following the man-ufacturer's instructions.

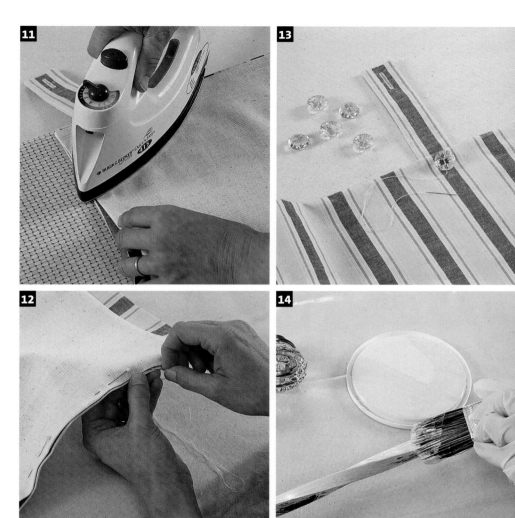

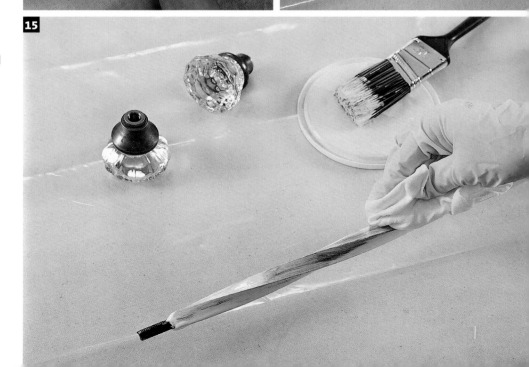

Decoupage Medallion

A VINTAGE TABLECLOTH from the homeowner's collection turned out to be the perfect fabric for the dining-chair cushions (see page 20). But before the cushions were stitched, portions of the tablecloth were photocopied on a color copier. The motifs were cut out and adhered to a medallion, a platelike surround for a ceiling-mounted light fixture. If you don't own a vintage tablecloth, use pieces of wallpaper or color copies of a reproduction fabric. (If you use wallpaper, peel apart the layers so the cutout shapes will be thin.)

MATERIALS

Latex paint in two colors

Paintbrush

Gloves

14-inch-diameter plastic ceiling medallion, available at home centers

Small, sharp scissors

Color photocopies of fabric or pieces of wallpaper

Decoupage finish (clear drying)

Foam brush

TIP

THIS LIGHT FIXTURE IS
REFERRED TO AS SEMIFLUSH
BECAUSE IT HANGS FROM
A STEM (ROD) A SHORT
DISTANCE FROM THE CEILING.
(FLUSH FIXTURES FIT
AGAINST THE CEILING, AND
PENDANTS HANG FARTHER
DOWN.) LOOK FOR A FIXTURE
WHOSE CANOPY (BASE) IS
FAIRLY SMALL SO IT WON'T
COVER UP THE MOTIFS ON
THE MEDALLION. IF YOU USE
A FIXTURE WITH A LARGE
CANOPY, PLACE THE MOTIFS
FARTHER FROM THE CENTER
OF THE MEDALLION.

Step by Step

1 Paint the face of the medallion the main color (yellow, on this medallion). Apply a second coat, if necessary. Allow the paint to dry. Paint the rim with the accent color.

2 Cut out the motifs, trimming off as much of the white (or other background color) as possible. Cut a variety of shapes, including some small, wispy ones. Arrange the motifs on the medallion, lapping a few onto the rim.

3 Working with one cutout at a time, use the foam brush to coat the backs of the motifs with decoupage finish, then press them to the medallion. Let the medallion dry. Brush with as many coats of the finish as needed to obscure the cut edges of the paper.

Scalloped Floorcloth

ANOTHER VINTAGE TABLECLOTH from the homeowner's collection took on a new role, this time underfoot as a floor covering. Plain canvas brushed with polyurethane provides the backing. Old-fashioned rickrack finishes the inner and outer edges and covers a multitude of sins, such as crooked lines and distorted edges sometimes found on vintage textiles. Colors are limited, so consider buying rickrack close to your desired color and painting it with acrylic craft paint. To clean the floorcloth, simply wipe it with a damp cloth.

TIP

THIS FLOORCLOTH RE-CEIVED A TOP COAT OF OIL-BASED POLYURETHANE, WHICH HAS A YELLOW CAST, TO ECHO THE WARM TONE OF THE PINE CABI-NETS. USE WATER-BASED POLYURETHANE TO MAIN-TAIN THE ORIGINAL COLOR OF THE FABRIC.

MATERIALS

Plastic drop cloth

10-ounce off-white
cotton canvas,
larger than the
tablecloth by several
inches on each side

Gloves

Water-based
polyurethane

Paintbrush
to apply
polyurethane

Vintage tablecloth or
other fabric

Brayer (roller),
available at paint and
craft stores

Rickrack

Acrylic paint and craft
brush (if you
paint the rickrack)

Gridded, nonwoven
pattern material,
available
at fabric stores

Rotary ruler
with 45-degree-angle
lines, available
at fabric stores and
quilt shops

Compass

Pins

Fabric scissors

Permanent fabric glue

Backing the Tablecloth

1 Cover your work surface with the plastic drop cloth. Lay the canvas on the drop cloth and smooth the wrinkles. Brush the canvas on one side with polyurethane, saturating the fabric. Work quickly; water-based polyurethane is fast drying.

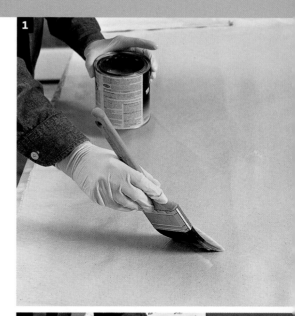

2 While the polyurethane is wet, carefully lay the tablecloth on top of the canvas. Position one edge of the cloth first, then smooth the fabric toward the opposite edge. Be sure to leave a small margin of canvas around the edges. (Having a helper hold one end makes this step easier.)

3 Brush a coat of polyurethane on the tablecloth, working from the center to the edges. Saturate the fabric, but do not leave puddles of polyurethane.

4 Use your hands and the brayer to adhere the fabric firmly to the canvas and to work any bubbles out to the edges. Allow to dry overnight.

Painting the Rickrack

5 Paint the rickrack with the acrylic paint if needed, one side at a time, allowing the first side to dry before you paint the other side.

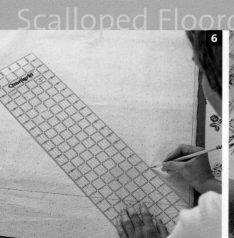

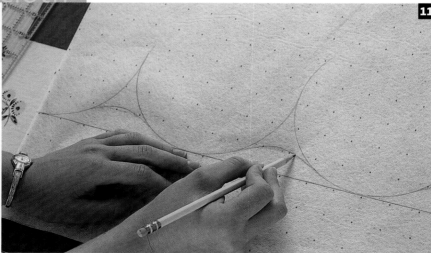

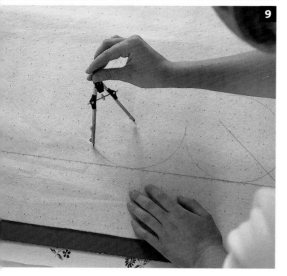

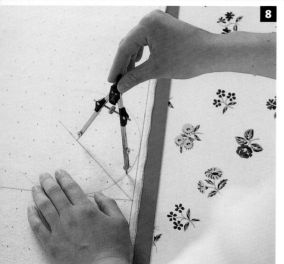

Making the Pattern

6 Determine the finished size you want your floorcloth to be. Fold the pattern material into quarters (once in half, then once again in half) and pin along the two folded edges to secure. From the folded point, measure and mark one-half the finished width on one folded edge and one-half the finished length on the other folded edge. (If your finished cloth will be a square, the measurement will be the same along both edges.) Draw lines marking the pattern edges. From the corner where the pattern lines intersect, use the rotary ruler to draw a line at a 45-degree angle inward about 10 inches.

7 Determine how many scallops you want along the edges; choose an odd number so you'll have a scallop centered at the midpoint of each edge. The edges of this square floorcloth each have seven scallops,

counting the ones in the corners. Then, follow the formula below to determine the size of the scallops. (If your floorcloth is rectangular, you'll need to figure the number and size of the scallops for the width and length separately; slight differences in scallop size will not be noticeable.)
A. Divide the number of scallops on one edge by 2. This is the number of scallops you will draw on the edge of the folded pattern material; it will include a half-scallop.
B. Divide the edge measurement on your pattern by the number you got in the preceding step. Round to the nearest fraction of an inch. This is the diameter of each scallop on that edge.

8 Set your compass to one-half the diameter of the scallop, determined in Step 7B. Position the compass point on the diagonal line you drew in Step 6 so that the lead arc just touches the pattern lines. Draw a near circle.

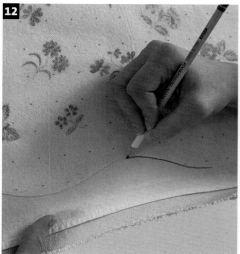

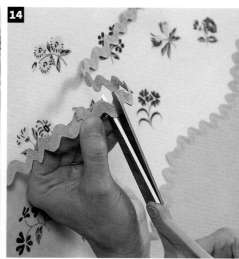

9 Working along one edge, toward the fold, lightly draw another scallop, positioning this scallop so it just touches the first scallop. Continue drawing scallops along the edge; you should end with a half-scallop at the fold.

10 Work along the other edge, again ending with a half-scallop at the fold.

11 Use a pencil to connect the scallops with gentle curves. Pin through all layers, close to the scalloped edges. Cut out the pattern through all thicknesses and unfold.

Trimming the Edges

12 Center the pattern on the floorcloth. If your floorcloth has motifs, use them as a guide. Draw around the pattern with a pencil, then cut out the floorcloth with fabric scissors.

13 About halfway between the midpoint of an edge and the corner, starting on an inside curve, run a bead of fabric glue along the cut edge for several inches. Leaving a few inches of rickrack free, lay the rickrack on the edge, over the glue, gently bending the trim as needed to fit the curves. Continue applying glue and rickrack almost all the way around the cut edge.

14 Stop gluing as you approach the starting point. On the inside curve, lay the ends of the rickrack on top of each other, over the cut edge of the floorcloth. Pinch the rickrack together and lift; cut through both layers at once with scissors. Finish gluing the rickrack, trimming the ends as needed so they butt together neatly. Add other rickrack accents, such as the inside border on this floorcloth, as desired. Apply another coat of polyurethane to the floorcloth, including the rickrack.

TIP

IT'S DIFFICULT TO GET THE SCALLOP SIZE AND PLACEMENT RIGHT THE FIRST TIME. TO AVOID ERASING ON THE PATTERN MATERIAL, FIRST DRAW THE SCALLOPS ON STRIPS OF TRACING PAPER TAPED TOGETHER AND LAID OVER THE PATTERN AT THE EDGES. (SECURE THE TRACING PAPER TO THE PATTERN WITH PINS OR TAPE.) WHEN YOU'VE GOT THE RIGHT-SIZE SCALLOP, DRAW THE SCALLOPS ON THE PATTERN.

New Looks for Vintage Materials

Tablecloth Cushions

FACING PAGE: **Dining-chair cushions—bordered, piped, and tied—showcase sections of a 1940s tablecloth. "Fussy cutting" the center square (isolating a major motif rather than cutting the tablecloth randomly) enhances the framed effect. The cushions are lightly filled with down.**

Flea Market Chandelier

BELOW: **The homeowner spied this chandelier, encrusted with paint and covered in dust, at a flea market. A cleanup, a fresh coat of paint, and a few replacement crystals brought it back to life.**

Clip-on Curtain

ABOVE: **Although it was delightful as a traditional rod-pocket curtain over the sink window (see the small photo on page 8), this kitchen linen looks even crisper pressed flat and hung with clip-on rings. The white-painted brackets and plain dowel blend with the window frame, keeping the focus on the metal rings and patterned curtain. The brackets are actually small wood candleholders (one of which was notched in the back so the dowel could snap in) screwed into the window frame laterally.**

Natural Charm

A TINY KITCHEN WITH CHARMING FEATURES—casement windows, custom-made cabinets, handsome wood floors, and a pass-through to an adjoining sunroom—needed mostly decorative touches. The homeowner's love of the natural world guided the design decisions. An ivy garland atop the main kitchen window softens the space and draws attention to the view. Stenciled tiles on the adjacent wall reiterate the natural theme, while a painted floorcloth puts a bit of color and pattern underfoot (see page 32). Most ambitious by far was the freestanding microwave cabinet (page 36), which keeps the counter uncluttered and lends a custom look to an everyday appliance.

A recent remodel, which included new tile and fresh paint, provided the ideal "blank canvas" for a variety of decorating projects in this kitchen and breakfast nook.

Vine and Ivy Garland

WHEN THERE'S LITTLE SPACE around a window and when privacy is not an issue, a natural window treatment like this one satisfies the desire for decoration and brings a bit of the outdoors inside. A garland is also an effective visual frame for a window that's too pretty to cover. This one is made from preserved ivy tucked into an unwound grapevine wreath. You can weave almost any living plant material into the grapevine to create a variety of seasonal looks, or use one of the many lifelike materials, such as stems of olive leaves or lavender, available at craft shops.

MATERIALS

Liquid glycerin, available at craft stores (read the warning label carefully)

Measuring cup

Bucket

Pruning shears

Lengths of ivy, each 3 to 4 feet long

Dried grapevine wreath, available at craft stores

Small hammer

Picture hangers

Florist's wire

Preparing the Ivy and Vine

1 Combine ½ cup of water and ½ cup of glycerin in the measuring cup; microwave the solution on "high" for 2 minutes to mix. Pour the mixture into the bucket. Cut the stem ends of the ivy; soak the ivy in the glycerin mixture for two to three days.

2 Soak the grapevine overnight in a tub of cold water. Unwind it, straightening the vine until it forms gentle curves.

Assembling the Window Treatment

3 Using a small hammer, install the picture hangers above the window. This window required three hangers, one at each corner and one in the center.

4 Use florist's wire to attach the vine to the hangers. Strive for asymmetrical balance, with one side of the vine longer than the other.

5 Tuck lengths of ivy into the vine, letting leafy ends trail down on each side.

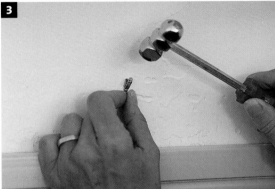

MATERIALS

Stencil plastic

Cutting mat

Craft knife

Repositionable spray adhesive

Four 13-inch-square ceramic tiles

4 ounces of latex glazing medium

Plastic plates

Opaque acrylic craft paint, three shades of green and one pewter, in 2-ounce bottles

Natural (sea) sponges

Paper towels

Steel tape measure

Contact cement

Heavy-duty ring hangers

DO IT TODAY

Stenciled Tiles

FOUR PEARS, EACH SLIGHTLY different, decorate the breakfast-nook wall. Limiting the paint colors to a narrow range of greens and hanging the ceramic tiles close together make for a cohesive look. Using paint in combination with glazing medium results in a lighter, more transparent effect. You can duplicate these designs using the patterns on pages 28 through 31 or modify designs from wrapping paper, wallpaper, or even fabric to make your own patterns.

FINISHED SIZE

27½ by 27½ inches for a grouping of four

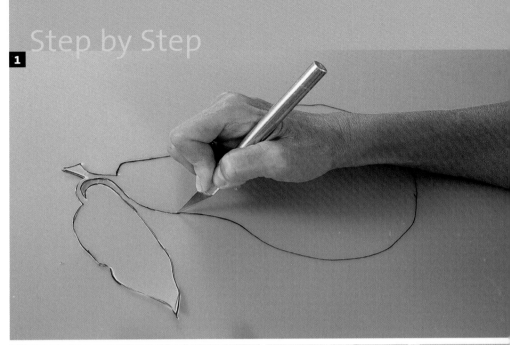

Stenciling the Tiles

1 Photocopy or trace the pear patterns. Lay stencil plastic over the patterns. Working on the cutting mat and using the craft knife, cut out the pears and the leaves.

2 Spray repositionable adhesive on the wrong side of a stencil; position the stencil on a tile and smooth to adhere it. Repeat to adhere stencils to the other tiles.

3 Pour four pools of glazing medium onto plastic plates. On top of each pool, pour a different paint color, using half as much paint as glazing medium. (You'll use the lighter greens and pewter for the interior of the pears and the darkest green on one edge to create the impression of a shadow.)

4 Dip a dry sponge into a paint-glaze mixture and dab the excess onto a paper towel.

5 Apply the paint to each tile through the stencil in a light up-and-down motion.

6 Remove the stencils. Before the paint dries, wet a paper towel and blot around the edges of the pears to soften the images.

Hanging the Tiles

7 Measure and mark the center of each tile approximately 3 inches from the upper edge.

8 Using the contact cement, glue the hangers to the backs, following the manufacturer's instructions.

9 Hang the tiles as a group, spacing them 1½ inches apart.

Pear patterns. See Step 1 on page 27.

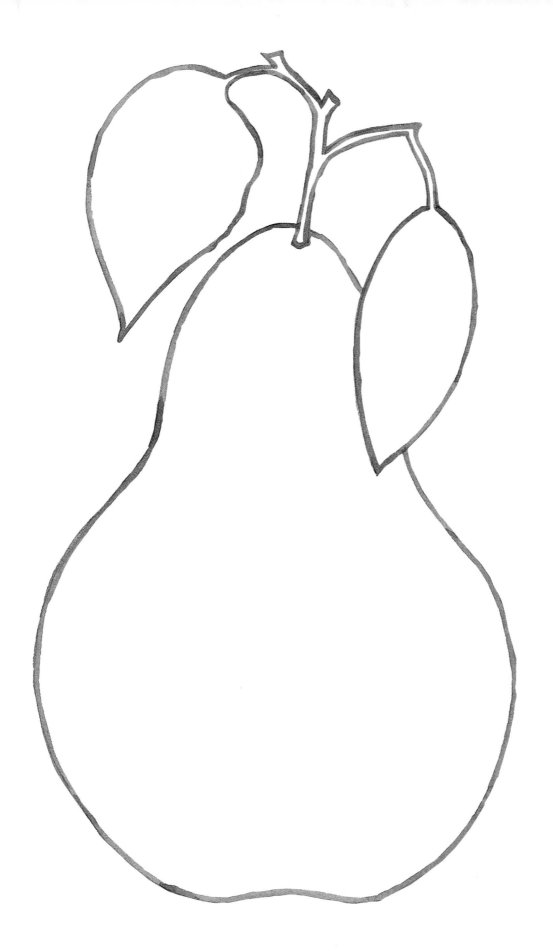

Pear patterns. See Step 1 on page 27.

MATERIALS

Scissors

1 yard of 10-ounce
cotton canvas,
natural color

Staple gun

Plywood, approximately
36 by 50 inches

Latex paint, satin finish,
pale yellow and white

Paintbrushes

Natural (sea) sponge

Paper towels

6- by 24-inch rotary
ruler, cutter, and cutting
mat, available at fabric
stores and quilt shops

¾-inch blue
painter's tape

2-inch foam brush

Opaque acrylic craft
paint: medium and dark
green, purple, and
yellow

Ceramic or glass plate

Grape leaves with stems

Craft brushes: ¼ inch,
⅜ inch, and ½ inch

Waxed paper

Brayer, available at paint
and craft stores

Water-based
polyurethane

Staple remover

DO IT TODAY

Fruits-of-the-Vine Floorcloth

THE HOMEOWNER'S AFFINITY for grapes, with their deep purple fruit and distinctive leaves, inspired this simple floorcloth. The leaf prints, termed monoprints because each leaf is used only once, are easy to create using acrylic paint and a printer's roller, known as a brayer. "Twirling" the grapes takes a bit of practice, but once you master the technique you'll find it useful for other decorative paint projects. The floorcloth wipes clean with a damp cloth.

FINISHED SIZE 23 by 37 inches

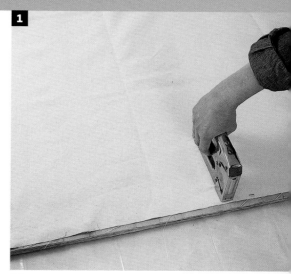

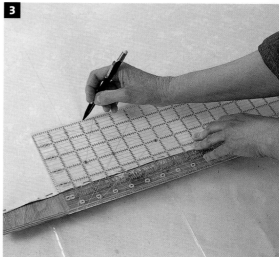

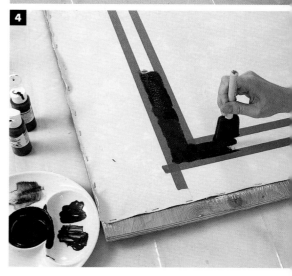

Painting the Background and Border

1 Cut the canvas to approximately 30 by 44 inches. Stretch and staple the canvas to the plywood as follows: place two staples at the midpoints of all the edges; then place single staples from the midpoints to the corners, working on one edge at a time and stretching the fabric evenly.

2 Paint the canvas with the pale yellow latex paint; allow to dry. Dip the sponge into the white latex paint; pounce (dab) the excess onto a paper towel, then dab the paint lightly and evenly onto the canvas.

3 To create the dark green border, measure and lightly mark a 22- by 36-inch rectangle in the center of the canvas. Measure and mark lines 1 inch inside the rectangle, forming a 1-inch-wide border.

4 Place blue painter's tape on the outside of the outer lines and inside of the inner lines. Using the foam brush and dark green acrylic paint, paint the border; allow to dry. Remove the tape.

Decorating the Floorcloth

5 Arrange the leaves on the canvas, mixing sizes and shapes. Group them in the corner, as shown, or place them around the border.

6 Carefully snip the stems from the leaves and set them aside. Brush medium green acrylic paint onto the back of a leaf.

7 Place the leaf, paint side down, on the floorcloth.

8 Cover the leaf with waxed paper and roll with the brayer, being careful not to shift the leaf as you work. Remove the waxed paper and lift the leaf. Repeat with the remaining leaves, using a clean piece of waxed paper each time.

9 To print each leaf stem, brush the back of a stem with green paint, place the stem at the base of the leaf print, and press with your fingers. Remove the stem.

10 Painting the grapes involves a two-step technique. First, with purple paint on a brush (¼- or ⅜-inch, depending on the size grape you want), push the brush straight down on the canvas, forcing the bristles to one side.

11 Second, keeping the brush straight up and down and firmly in place, twirl it to make a painted circle.

12 Using the ¼-inch brush, accent the leaves with the yellow paint.

Finishing the Floorcloth

13 Apply two coats of water-based polyurethane, allowing the floorcloth to dry after each coat. Using a staple remover, remove the canvas from the plywood.

14 Use the dark green border as a reference point to trim the edges as follows: On the painted side of the floorcloth, measure and lightly mark a line ½ inch beyond the outer edge of the dark green border and another line 2½ inches from the outer edge of the border. Trim the floorcloth with scissors on the outer line.

15 Turn the floorcloth over; from the cut edges, measure and mark lines at 2 inches and 4 inches, continuing the lines to the edges of the canvas. The overlapping lines should create four squares in each corner.

16 At each corner, use the ruler to mark a 45-degree-angle line passing diagonally through the center of the squares; trim the corner as shown at top right.

17 Fold the edges in to meet the inner marked lines, forming a miter in the hem at each corner.

18 Finger-press the edges and turn the floorcloth right side up.

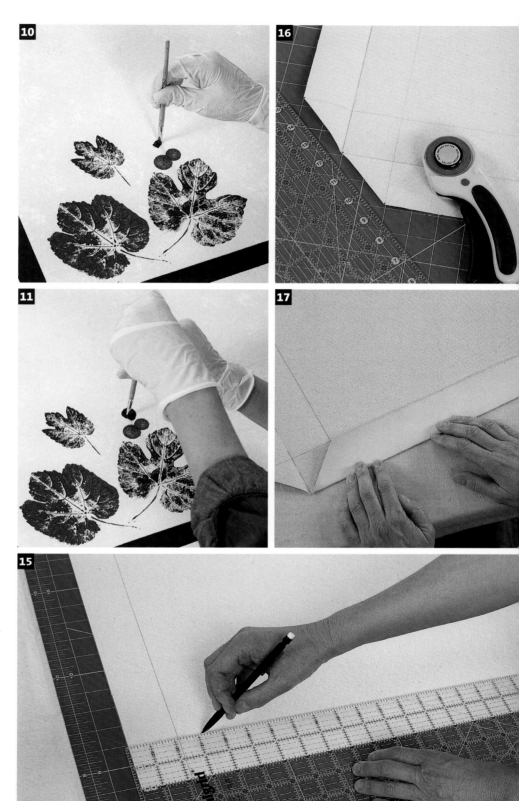

MATERIALS

4- by 8-foot sheet of ¾-inch MDF, cut into three 18- by 29½-inch pieces and one 19⅞- by 33¼-inch piece, plus scraps

Four supports, each 2½ by 2½ by 15¾ inches

Electric drill

Wood screws: four 2-inch, eight 2½-inch, ten 1¼-inch, thirty-nine ¾-inch, and six ½-inch

Drill bits: ⅜-inch brad-point bit, ⅜-inch spade bit, ⁷⁄₁₆-inch drill bit

Four nails

Four turned table legs, each 2½ inches square at the top and 23¾ inches long

Handsaw

10 feet of ⅜-inch doweling

Wood glue

Hammer

Hole saw

Sharp chisel

Wood scraps for shims

12 feet of ¾-inch cove molding

WOOD SHOP

Microwave Cabinet

THE MICROWAVE, one of the most-used appliances in the kitchen, can swallow up a lot of space. A freestanding cabinet like the one shown here efficiently houses a microwave, frees up valuable counter area, and adds a look of custom furniture to a kitchen. This project requires intermediate woodworking skills. Have the shelf pieces, upper supports, and turned legs cut at a woodworking or cabinet shop; ask for the scraps.

FINISHED SIZE 33¼ inches wide, 19⅞ inches deep, 41¾ inches tall

Materials list

Miter box and backsaw

Metal ruler, 12 inches long and 1 inch wide

Electric brad nailer with 1-inch nails, or hammer and finishing nails

36 inches of wicker webbing, 24 inches wide

4 by 4 feet of ¼-inch plywood, plus scraps

Foam roller

Wood clamps

Utility knife

Steel measuring tape

6 feet of 2-inch molding

12 feet of 1-inch molding

6 feet of ⅜-inch copper tubing

Hacksaw or tubing cutter

Tubing bender

Sandpaper, 60- and 120-grit

Fly cutter with drill press

12 feet of 8-gauge copper wire

Latex primer and paint

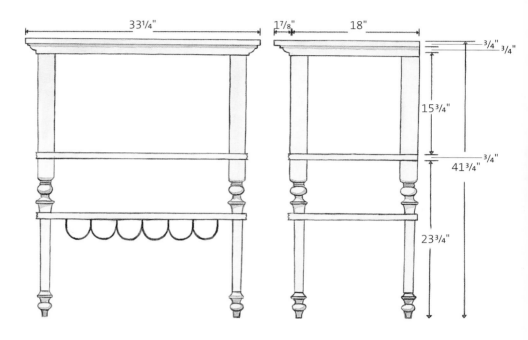

Front and side views illustrate the dimensions of this cabinet and its components. See the tip below to change the dimensions to fit your microwave.

TIP THIS CABINET WAS DESIGNED FOR A MICROWAVE THAT MEASURES 23½ INCHES WIDE, 17 INCHES DEEP, AND 13¾ INCHES HIGH. IF YOUR MICROWAVE IS A DIFFERENT SIZE, ADD 6 INCHES TO ITS WIDTH AND 1 INCH TO ITS DEPTH TO DETERMINE THE CUT MEASUREMENTS FOR THE THREE MDF SHELF PIECES. FOR THE TOP (LARGEST) MDF PIECE, ADD ANOTHER 3¾ INCHES TO THE WIDTH (THE LONG EDGE) AND 1⅞ INCHES TO THE DEPTH TO DETERMINE THE CUT MEASUREMENT. ADD 2 INCHES TO THE HEIGHT OF YOUR MICROWAVE TO DETERMINE THE CUT MEASUREMENT OF THE UPPER SUPPORTS.

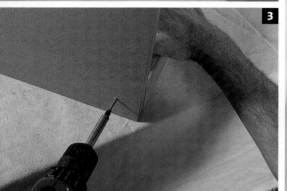

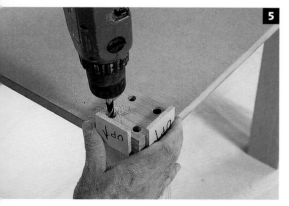

Constructing the Basic Cabinet

1 Mark each corner of an 18- by 29½-inch MDF piece with a different letter. Mark each of the four 2½- by 2½- by 15¾-inch supports with one of those letters. These pieces will form the microwave shelf and upper supports; the letters will allow you to match the pieces as you construct the unit.

2 Using the electric drill, predrill a hole in each corner of the shelf piece 1¼ inches from the edges.

3 With the shelf piece on its side and one upper support resting on the work surface, flush with the edges of the shelf, screw the shelf to the support using a 2-inch wood screw (enlist a helper to hold the pieces flush while you screw them together). Repeat with the remaining three supports on the other corners of the shelf.

4 Use a scrap of MDF 2½ inches square, the electric drill, and the ³⁄₈-inch brad-point bit to make a jig for drilling four holes for dowels; exact spacing between the holes isn't critical. Nail scraps of MDF or wood to two edges and mark with directional arrows as shown. (Because you'll be drilling into the *bottom* of the supports and the *top* of the turned legs, you'll need to flip the jig to make the holes match.)

5 Place the shelf so it's standing on all four supports. (The shelf is actually upside down in this position.) Set the jig in a corner, with the arrows pointing down, as shown at bottom left on the facing page. With the brad-point bit, drill holes for the dowels through the shelf and into the upper support. Remove the jig and finish drilling to 2⅝ inches. (To ensure you drill to the proper depth, wrap a piece of tape around the bit at 2⅝ inches, leaving the tape ends stuck together out to the side. When the flap of tape sweeps away the sawdust, you'll know you've drilled to the correct depth.) Repeat on the other corners.

6 Remove the jig and turn it in the other direction, with the arrows pointing up, and place it on the square top of one of the turned legs. Mark the outside corner of the leg (the corner framed by the overhanging jig pieces). Drill dowel holes 2⅝ inches into the turned leg. Repeat on the remaining turned legs.

7 Using the handsaw, cut 20 dowels, each 5 inches long. You'll use four for each corner and four to secure the bottom shelf.

8 Squeeze wood glue into the dowel holes in the shelf and upper support at one corner and push the dowels into the holes far enough so that a little glue oozes up.

9 Insert all four dowels as far in as they will go, tapping them with a hammer if necessary to get them to the same level. Work efficiently; wood glue dries quickly. Repeat on the remaining corners.

10 Put glue into the dowel holes on one of the turned legs. Flip the leg upside down and onto the dowels, placing the outside corner of the leg (marked in Step 6) on the corner of the shelf-support unit. Tap the leg down if necessary. Repeat on the remaining corners.

11 Measure the diameter of the turned part of a leg at the point where you want the shelf to be. Using a hole saw as large as that diameter, cut holes in another 18- by 29½-inch MDF piece so it will fit over the legs. These holes must be precisely centered in 2½-inch-square areas at the corners of the shelf to make them align with the 2½-inch-square tops of the legs. Use scraps of MDF to support the shelf as you cut the holes.

12 With the unit upside down, slide the shelf with the holes over the turned legs. Use the chisel to cut shims from wood scraps; slip the shims into the holes to keep the legs centered and snug.

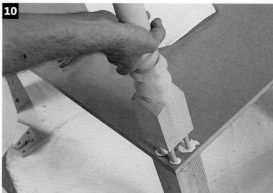

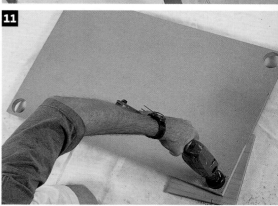

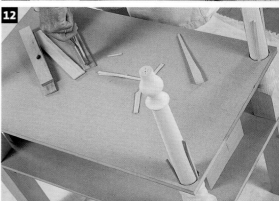

MDF piece on the upper supports. Screw through the top shelf and into the legs, using two 2½-inch wood screws in each corner, as shown.

Adding the Sides and Top

18 On one side of the cabinet, measure the distance from support to support and from top shelf to microwave shelf to determine the lengths of ¾-inch cove molding needed to frame the wicker insets. Cut the molding pieces, mitering the corners using the miter box.

13 Position the drill, fitted with a ³/₈-inch spade bit, precisely at one corner of the shelf, perfectly parallel to the floor. To ensure that your drill is level, have someone sight it from the side.

14 Drill through the MDF, through the leg, and into the MDF again.

15 Put wood glue into the hole and insert a dowel as far as it will go. Trim the dowel flush with the corner, using a handsaw.

16 Using the chisel and a light touch, trim the shims flush with the shelf. Leave the shims in place. Insert dowels in the remaining corners and trim in the same way.

17 Stand the unit on its legs. Place the remaining 18- by 29½-inch

19 Lay the inch-wide metal ruler flat along the edge of the microwave shelf as a placement guide for the bottom piece of molding.

20 Using the brad nailer (or a hammer and finishing nails), attach the cove molding to the shelf,

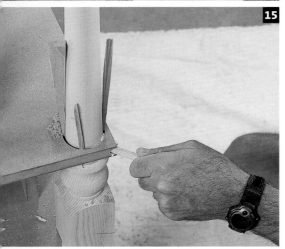

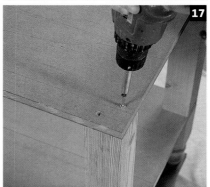

angling the nails through the center of the molding and into the shelf at the ends and every 4 inches.

21 Position and attach the remaining pieces of molding in the same way. Repeat on the other side of the cabinet.

22 To make the wicker insets that fit behind the molding, cut the wicker and plywood to the dimensions determined in Step 18. Use the foam roller to apply wood glue to one side of the plywood and the back side of the wicker; put the two pieces together, cover the wicker with large pieces of sturdy cardboard and plywood, and clamp. Allow the glue to dry; trim the ragged edges of the wicker with the utility knife.

23 From inside the cabinet, fit the wicker insets against the molding; install a ¾-inch wood screw through the plywood and wicker and into the back of the molding piece on each side.

24 Place the cabinet upside down on the 19⅞- by 33¼-inch piece of MDF. Position the back of the cabinet flush with a long edge of the MDF (there's no reveal on the back). Use a steel tape to center the unit and maintain an even reveal on the sides.

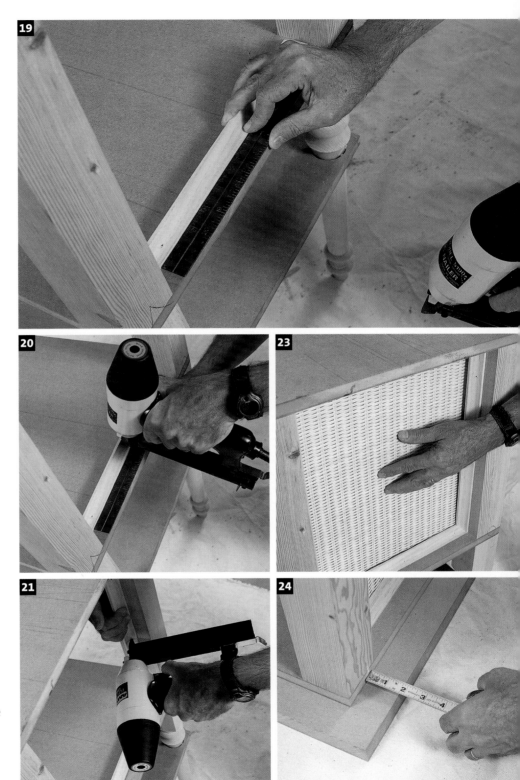

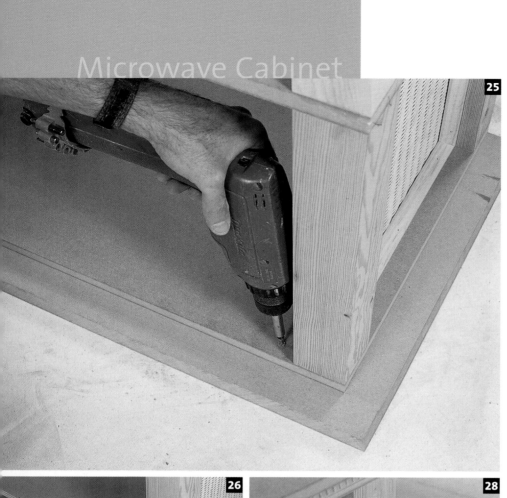

25 Screw the underside of the top shelf to the 19⁷⁄₈- by 33¼-inch piece with 1¼-inch wood screws, placing one in each corner, two evenly spaced along the front and back, and one centered on each side.

26 Measure, mark, and cut the 2-inch molding for the upper edge of the cabinet, mitering the corners using the miter box. Glue and brad-nail (or hammer, with finishing nails) the molding to the edges as shown.

27 Repeat with the 1-inch molding on the two lower shelves.

Attaching the Towel Rack

28 Place the cabinet right side up. On the side supports, measure 8 inches down from the underside of the top. Make a mark, centered, on each support.

29 Drill a hole, ⁷⁄₁₆ inch in diameter and 1½ inches deep, at the mark on each support to accept the ³⁄₈-inch copper tubing.

30 Cut the copper tubing into two 22-inch lengths. Using the tubing bender, form each length into a towel rack that measures approximately 15½ inches wide.

31 Scuff up the ends of the tubing with 60-grit sandpaper so it will accept the wood glue. Put glue into the holes and slip in the tubing.

Attaching the Wine Rack

32 Using a fly cutter with a drill press, cut six circles, each 3½ inches in diameter, to make a jig for the wine-rack loops. Space the circles 4 inches apart, measuring from center to center, and screw them into scrap plywood using ½-inch wood screws. Add ¾-inch wood screws on either side of the circles, 4¼ inches above their lower edge. Wrap copper wire over and under the screws and wood circles, looping the ends around the outer screws. Trim the excess wire; unhook the wire from the screws. Use the jig and another length of copper wire to form a second series of loops.

33 Place the cabinet upside down. On the lower shelf, center the first loops 4 inches from the front edge. Secure with ¾-inch wood screws on both sides of each wire bend, as shown, screwing them just partway in. Center and attach the second loops 10 inches from the front edge.

34 Finish turning the screws by hand to avoid overtightening.

Finishing the Cabinet

35 Sand the cabinet with 120-grit sandpaper, then prime and paint it.

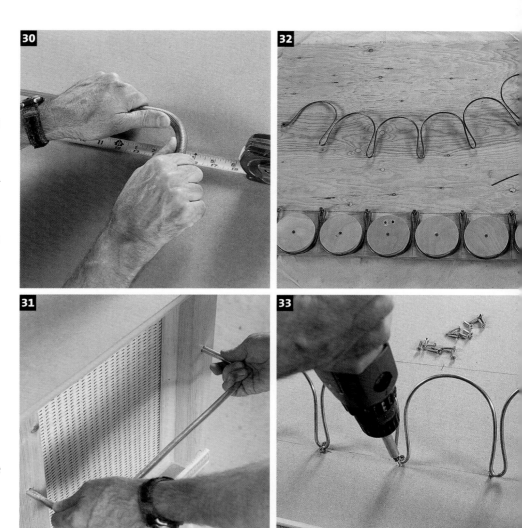

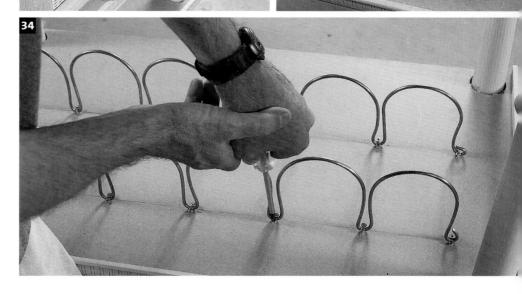

43

MATERIALS

Latex primer

½-inch MDF, large
enough to accommo-
date the table, plus sev-
eral inches on all sides

Circular saw

Metal straightedge

Molding equal in length
to the perimeter of the
table, plus 2 feet

Adjustable miter box

Wood glue

Electric brad nailer with
nails to attach the molding

Wood putty

100-grit sandpaper

Latex paint to
match the table

6- by 24-inch
rotary ruler

¾-inch blue
painter's tape

Opaque acrylic craft
paint in three shades of
green, plus yellow

2-inch foam brush

⅝-inch stencil brush

Grape or maple leaves

Waxed paper

Brayer

Water-based
polyurethane and
paintbrush

IN A WEEKEND

Removable Tabletop

IF YOU'RE LUCKY ENOUGH to have a piece of furniture that's been handed down through your family, you may be reluctant to make dramatic changes in its appearance. A simple solution for an antique table is to make a separate top that fits over the existing table. A lip of molding around the edges holds the tabletop in place. Painter's tape makes it easy to create a near-perfect checkerboard design.

Making the Tabletop

1 Prime the MDF. Center your table upside down on it. Stand a straight, ½-inch-wide board or piece of MDF on its side, flush with one edge of the table. Using the board as a guide, draw a line the length of the table side onto the MDF.

2 Mark all the sides in the same way, making sure you don't shift the table. The width of the board will result in a tabletop that's slightly larger than the original table, allowing it to fit easily over the table.

3 Cut out the tabletop with the circular saw.

4 To get the angles for the miter cuts you'll make in the molding, use the metal straightedge to draw lines connecting opposite points on the tabletop, creating pie-shaped segments. (The sides of an octagonal table may have slightly different angles at the points; connecting opposite points ensures accurate miters.) Number the segments 1 through 8.

5 Hold the molding upside down against one edge of the marked tabletop as shown. (The facedown surface of the table is the top.) Align the straightedge with one of the lines you drew in Step 4. Continue the line onto the molding.

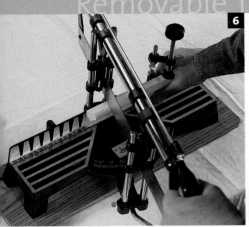

6 With the molding standing upright, align the line you just drew on the molding with the blade on the adjustable miter box. Clamp the molding in place; cut it with the backsaw.

7 Place the molding against the corresponding edge of the tabletop, aligning the angle you just cut with the drawn line. Mark the angle on the other end of the molding the same way you marked the first end.

8 Cut the other end of the molding with the miter box. Label the inside of the molding with the segment number. Cut and mark the

remaining pieces of molding in the same way.

9 Glue the molding pieces to the edges, lining them up precisely. Use the brad nailer to attach the molding to the sides.

10 Fill any holes with wood putty. Sand and prime the tabletop, then paint it to match the table.

Decorating the Tabletop

11 To create a checkerboard pattern, measure and mark a 16-inch square, centered, on the MDF top. Tape the outsides of the square

using painter's tape. Press firmly on the inner edges of the tape to prevent paint from seeping under.

12 Starting at one edge of the square, use the rotary ruler to make marks on the tape every 2 inches. Repeat on the remaining edges. Connect the marks on opposite edges to create eight rows of 2-inch squares.

13 Paint the 16-inch square with light green acrylic paint and the foam brush. If you use a darker color that obscures the grid lines, you'll still have the marks on the tape to guide you.

14 In preparation for painting the odd-numbered rows in the checkerboard pattern, first place a piece of tape below the top horizontal line you drew, with the edge of the tape on the line as shown.

15 Place another piece of tape above the second line (you should now have a ½-inch gap between the two pieces of tape). Tape below the third line and above the fourth line and so on down

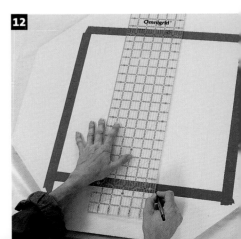

the painted square, ending with tape below the seventh line.

16 Tape the vertical lines as follows: Working from the right edge of the square, place a piece of tape on the left side of the first marked vertical line. Place the next piece of tape on the right side of the second vertical line. Tape on the left side of the third line, the right side of the fourth line, and so on, ending with tape on the left side of the seventh line.

17 Load your stencil brush with medium green paint; pounce (dab) the brush on a paper towel to remove the excess. Starting in the upper-right corner of the taped area, paint the first four 2-inch squares in the top row, working from right to left. Leave the fifth space unpainted.

18 Move to the third row (the next row with 2-inch squares showing) and repeat the process, starting by painting the far-right square and ending with an unpainted space. Repeat for the fifth and seventh rows. Let the paint dry.

19 Carefully remove the vertical pieces of tape, then remove the horizontal pieces. Leave the perimeter tape in place.

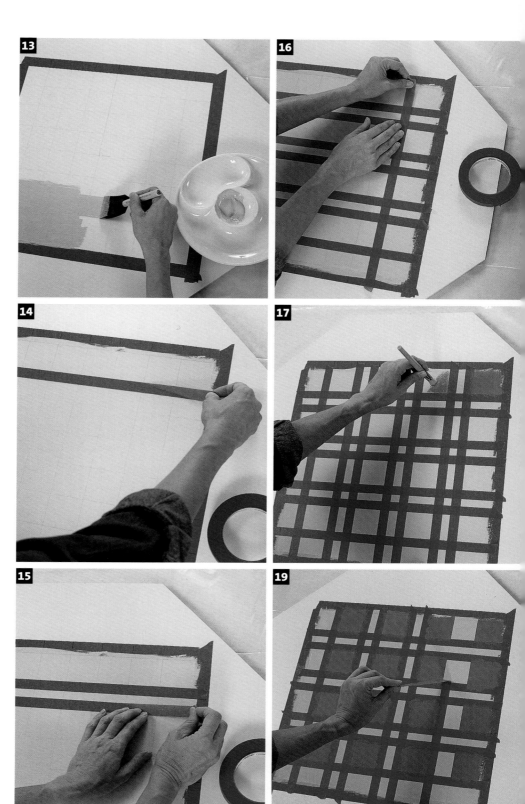

to the upper-right square in the first row), then paint every other square, working from right to left. The last square in the row will be painted. Continue painting the rest of the even-numbered rows in the same manner. Allow the paint to dry. Remove the vertical pieces of tape, then the horizontal pieces.

23 Remove the tape surrounding the checkerboard.

24 Using the rotary ruler, lightly mark lines ¼ inch from the edges of the checkerboard. Tape on the outside of these lines; also tape on the edges of the checkerboard.

25 Using your stencil brush, paint the border dark green. Allow the paint to dry. Remove the tape.

Finishing the Tabletop

26 To print leaves around the checkerboard, see the "Fruits-of-the-Vine Floorcloth," Steps 6 through 9, on page 34.

27 Apply two coats of water-based polyurethane to the tabletop's surface and the molding, allowing the first coat to dry before applying the second.

20 Tape lines again, this time in preparation for painting the even-numbered rows. Start with the horizontal lines: Tape above the first marked line and below the second line. Tape above the third line, below the fourth line, and so on, ending with tape above the seventh line.

21 Next, tape the vertical lines, starting from the left edge. Tape to the right of the first vertical line and to the left of the second line. Tape to

the right of the third line and to the left of the fourth line and so on, ending with tape to the right of the seventh line.

HINT: It may help if you keep in mind that with this round of taping, you'll put the tape over the squares you've already painted.

22 Starting with the second row, paint the second 2-inch square from the right (this square is kitty-corner

Decorative Details

Wood Accents

ABOVE: **A custom-made cornice and plate rack add fine detailing to the cabinets and frame the pass-through.**

Bin Drawers

BELOW: **Mixed pasta, dried chilies, and bay leaves fill the shallow display fronts on bin drawers and inject color and pattern into the neutral scheme. For variety, the homeowner changes the contents.**

Metal Sconces

Candle sconces do double duty, covering the original, nonfunctioning electrical plates and repeating the leafy patterns in the kitchen and the adjacent sunroom.

Quiet Color

ABOVE: A pale palette of yellow, green, off-white, and taupe, anchored by a charcoal gray slate floor, repeats the kitchen color scheme. The octagonal table, a family treasure, was painted to match the microwave cabinet, then scrubbed with fine steel wool to give it a slightly worn look.

Tufted Cushions

ABOVE: **A damask tablecloth with a grape-leaf pattern was cut and sewn into cushions for the wicker chairs. Originally dark, the chairs were painted to match the creamy background color of the fabric, brightening the space.**

Living Window

LEFT: **A hummingbird bush *(Grevillea thelemanniana)* wends its way around the corner windows, contributing graceful pattern and natural color.**

Surface Appeal

INSPIRED BY THE HUSHED HUES and natural materials of Tuscany, the owner-designer of this light-filled kitchen and dining area followed a decorating plan that incorporated a range of sophisticated colors and appealing textures. Walls the color of summer straw look and feel like authentic fresco; neutral granite tile possesses visual, rather than actual, texture. The island—wallpapered with brown bags, then tinted and waxed—brings to mind the warmth of old leather. The delight is in the details, as well: turned legs under the island counter, decorative glass in cabinet doors, and new stainless-steel "skins" on the existing dishwasher.

With its open plan and abundant windows, this kitchen hardly qualified as a "problem room," but it was not living up to its potential.

MATERIALS

Masking tape/
paper dispenser

Drop cloths

Gloves

Universal tint, in
yellow oxide, available
at home centers and
paint stores

Latex primer

Paint roller

Low-nap roller covers
(¼ or ⅜ inch)

Two 2-inch tapered
brushes (almost any size
will work)

Two 2-gallon buckets
with lids

One 12-pound tub of
all-purpose, ready-mixed
joint compound,
available at home
centers and paint stores

Metal drywall-taping
knives (don't use
plastic ones)

Kitchen sponges

Small bucket for
fresh water

Spray bottle with
a fine-mist nozzle

Water-based
polyurethane

Roller or paintbrush to
apply polyurethane

IN A WEEKEND

Fresco Walls

THIS DECORATIVE PAINT TECHNIQUE, reminiscent of Italian fresco, uses mixtures of paint tint and joint compound to add mottled color and irresistible texture to plain walls. On the practical side, this treatment camouflages damaged surfaces and is easy to apply, even for beginners. (If you're new to decorative paint techniques, enlist the help of a friend to make the job go faster.) The joint compound is water based, making it workable for at least 15 minutes.

TIP

ONCE YOU START WORKING WITH THE COMPOUND, KEEP SCRAPING THE INSIDES OF THE BUCKETS CLEAN. IF YOU DON'T, DRY CHUNKS OF COMPOUND WILL FALL INTO THEM, CAUSING STREAKS WHEN YOU PAINT. WHEN YOU'RE NOT USING THE COMPOUND, SPRAY THE SURFACE OF IT WITH A FINE MIST OF WATER, COVER WITH PLASTIC WRAP, AND PUT THE LIDS ON.

Applying the Primer

1 Tape off the ceiling, cabinets, and any other surface or area you want to protect. Lay drop cloths on the floor.

2 Using the universal tint, tint the primer to a light version of the color you desire. (Your paint source can also tint the primer for you.)

3 Roll the primer over large areas to create an undercoat for the joint compound; use a tapered brush to apply the primer to small areas. Allow the primer to dry.

Applying the Joint Compound

4 Using the universal tint, mix two, different-colored batches of the joint compound in the 2-gallon buckets, varying the value (the lightness or darkness) of the colors as desired. If necessary, add a small amount of water to the compound to make it the consistency of spreadable cake frosting.

5 Skim a coat of the lighter compound onto the wall with a taping knife, working in different directions and overlapping your strokes. Strive to get the compound off the knife and onto the wall, rather than just scraping it across the surface. Alternate with the darker compound. Work in a small area, then move to the next area, until the entire surface is covered.

6 Using a damp sponge and a wiping action, smooth and manipulate the compound until you create a slightly raised surface. If the mixture has dried too much to move, spray the surface with a fine mist of water and gently work it with the sponge.

Sealing the Walls

7 Allow the surface to dry thoroughly. Temperature and humidity will affect the drying time of the compound; thicker areas will take considerably longer to dry.

8 Roll or brush on two coats of polyurethane, following the manufacturer's instructions.

Island Legs

ADDING LEGS TO AN ISLAND and breakfast bar is a great way to introduce the look of freestanding furniture to your kitchen. Legs can also make an island appear larger—a pleasing spatial illusion in almost any kitchen area. You may finish the legs to match the sides of your island, but they'll convey the feel of furniture more effectively if they're of a contrasting color and texture. These legs were added after the island's old surface was removed, so they could be secured to the underlayment before the new surface was laid.

MATERIALS

Two 3½-inch-diameter table legs equal in length to the height of the island, available from home centers and through woodworking catalogs

Carpenter's level

Combination or carpenter's square

Circular saw

Electric drill and drill bit

Six wood screws

Preparing the Legs

1 If you plan to paint the legs, prime them now. If you plan to finish them another way, do that now. (These legs were later painted yellow to match the walls, then waxed; for waxing instructions, see Steps 10 and 11 on page 69.)

2 Remove the fascia board on one end of the island so you can see the underside of the countertop, called the underlayment. (You will be able to slip both legs into position from the one open end.)

3 Position a leg next to the exposed end of the island; use a level to make sure it's straight up and down. With a combination or carpenter's square, draw a line on the leg even with the bottom of the underlayment, as shown. Repeat to mark the second leg.

4 Cut the legs on the marked lines.

Securing the Legs to the Floor

5 Put each leg in place under the counter, again using the level to make sure it's straight. Lightly draw around the base of each leg where it touches the floor. Remove the legs.

6 Predrill a hole, centered, in the bottom of each leg. Insert a wood screw, leaving ³/₈ inch of it exposed.

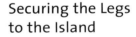

7 In the middle of each circle drawn on the floor, drill a hole slightly larger than the head of the wood screw and to the depth of the exposed screw.

8 Insert the screw heads into the holes and fit the legs under the island, positioning the farther leg first.

Securing the Legs to the Island

9 Use the level to make sure each leg is straight up and down; then, working from the top of the island, screw two screws through the underlayment and into each leg. Reattach the fascia board.

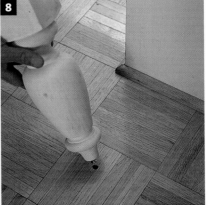

MATERIALS

Eye and ear protection

⅝-inch chisel and hammer

Electric sander with
80-grit sandpaper

Utility knife and metal
straightedge

Ceramic tile backerboard
and screws

Electric drill and
combination countersink–
pilot hole drill bit

Thinset adhesive

¼- by ⅜-inch
square-notched trowel

Lightweight and
heavyweight gloves

Graph paper

Granite tile

Blue painter's tape

Diamond-blade wet saw

Steel tape measure

Tile spacers to match
the grout width (see the
tip on page 63)

Carpenter's level

Silicone sealant

Varathane

Grout and caulk
(see the tip on page 63)

Grout float

Bucket and sponges

Granite and grout sealer

MAKEOVER MAGIC

Granite Tile Counter

GRANITE SLAB IS ONE OF THE MOST EXQUISITE countertop surfaces—with a price to match its beauty. Fortunately, granite tile is a less expensive alternative, and setting the tile is an easy do-it-yourself project. The steps that follow are for this kitchen's island (the completed island is shown on page 66). As you can see, the sink counter and backsplashes were also tiled. If you plan to tile the backsplashes, do them last.

TIP

YOU CAN USE SOME TILES WHOLE, BUT YOU'LL UNDOUBTEDLY NEED TO TRIM SOME TO FIT YOUR COUNTER. FOR THIS JOB, YOU CAN RENT A SPECIAL TILE-CUTTING SAW, CALLED A WET SAW, FROM TILE SUPPLIERS, HOME CENTERS, AND EQUIPMENT-RENTAL STORES. TAKE THE TIME YOU NEED TO LEARN TO USE A WET SAW. WHEN YOU BUY YOUR TILE, ASK FOR CHIPPED OR BROKEN PIECES ON WHICH TO PRACTICE MAKING CUTS.

Removing the Existing Tile

If you're tiling a new island, skip to Step 5.

1 Wearing eye protection, use your chisel and hammer to crack the island surface, starting in the center of a tile.

2 Slide the chisel under the tile, lifting the pieces and removing the adhesive down to the plywood underlayment.

3 Slide the chisel under an adjoining tile and lift it. Remove all tiles in this manner. (If you plan to reuse the counter trim, be careful not to damage it as you remove the tiles.)

4 To remove the trim, place a scrap of wood at one inside corner and tap to loosen the joint. Tap the trim piece at 1-foot increments, easing the trim out from the counter by a consistent distance to prevent splitting the trim. Repeat to remove all the trim. Mark each piece so you'll know where it goes when you reattach it.

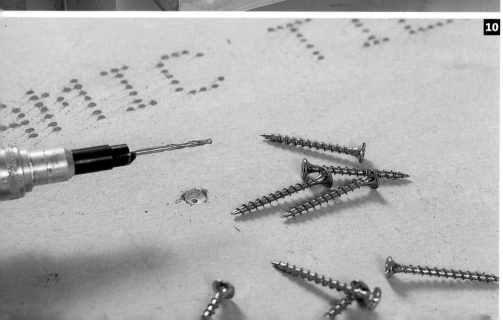

Preparing the Surface

5 Using the electric sander with 80-grit sandpaper, sand off the existing adhesive to level the underlayment surface.

6 Using the utility knife and metal straightedge, measure and cut the backerboard to fit the counter. Predrill holes in the backerboard where marked, using the combination countersink–pilot hole drill bit.

7 Prepare the thinset according to the manufacturer's instructions. Using the smooth side of your notched trowel, spread the thinset over the entire surface of the island to within ½ inch of the counter edges.

8 Holding the wide notched side of the trowel at a 30-degree angle, spread the thinset over the surface, creating ridges (see photos 8 and 9). Strive to leave ridges approximately two-thirds the depth of the trowel notches.

9 Set the backerboard in place, pushing it down with medium pressure.

10 Screw the backerboard in place through the predrilled holes and into the counter, making sure to countersink the screws.

11 Hold the trim against the corresponding edges and draw a pencil line along each length, marking the backerboard. This line will be the outer grout line. Set the trim pieces aside again. Then, at the desired grout width (1/8 inch on this project), carefully mark the inner grout line.

Planning the Layout

12 A standard approach to planning tile for a rectangular counter that's not interrupted by a sink or stovetop is to use a complete tile in each corner, then adjust the size of the remaining tiles to fit. (For a counter with a sink or drop-in stove, remove the sink or stovetop before planning and installing tile.)

13 On graph paper, draw your countertop to scale and sketch the tile layout, allowing for the grout lines between tiles and around the edges. Number the drawn tiles and include directional arrows for grain line or pattern if the tile has either. Label each full tile to be cut with a piece of blue tape marked with the tile number and orientation.

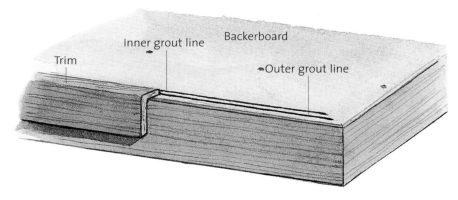

Inner grout line   Backerboard

Trim   Outer grout line

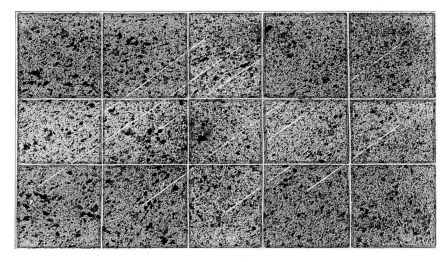

Complete tiles are shaded; the others needed to be cut to fit.

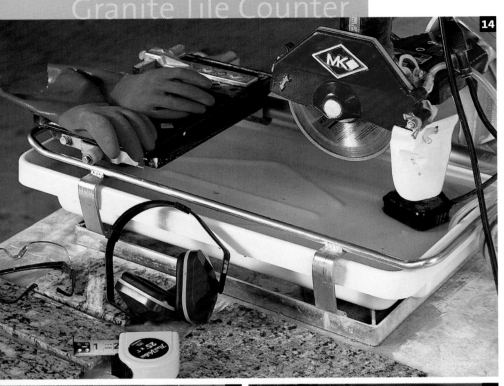

Cutting the Tile

14 Gather the tools you will need to cut the tile with the wet saw: heavyweight gloves, eye and ear protection, and a steel tape measure.

15 Set the wet saw's fence (the piece that guides the tile during cutting) to the desired tile width, as indicated on the measurement bar. Use the steel tape to check the accuracy of the bar by holding one end of the tape against the fence and the other at the desired tile width. If the measurement on the bar is not exactly correct, you'll need to adjust the fence.

16 Remove the tape label from your first tile. With the finished side of the granite up, cut the tile. (Cutting on this side minimizes chipping.) Don't force the tile; if sparks fly, you are pushing too hard. Use a gentle touch, allowing the blade to grind through the tile. When you're

Angled Cuts

The tile for the backsplash in the bay window of this kitchen required angled cuts because the homeowner didn't want wide grout lines; see the photo on page 58. You can make angled cuts for mitered corners by tilting the blade on the wet saw. When making an angled cut, hold the tile against the fence as you would for any other cut.

see the photo on page 58.

finished cutting the tile, re-place the tape, with the arrow going in the correct direction. (If you chip a tile, use a fragment from other cut tiles or use tile nippers to break off a piece to fit the chipped area. Set the tile as planned, then use silicone sealant to put the fragment in place.)

17 Cut the remaining tiles, replacing the tape labels immediately after cutting.

Setting the Tile

18 Before you set the tile, do a dry-run layout on the counter, using tile spacers at each corner to ensure that the tiles meet at right angles. Check the location of the numbered tiles against your layout drawing. Recut tiles if necessary for an accurate fit. Remove the tiles.

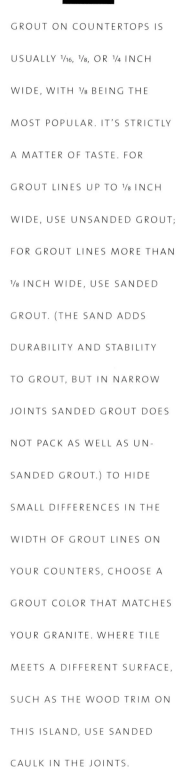

TIP

GROUT ON COUNTERTOPS IS USUALLY $\frac{1}{16}$, $\frac{1}{8}$, OR $\frac{1}{4}$ INCH WIDE, WITH $\frac{1}{8}$ BEING THE MOST POPULAR. IT'S STRICTLY A MATTER OF TASTE. FOR GROUT LINES UP TO $\frac{1}{8}$ INCH WIDE, USE UNSANDED GROUT; FOR GROUT LINES MORE THAN $\frac{1}{8}$ INCH WIDE, USE SANDED GROUT. (THE SAND ADDS DURABILITY AND STABILITY TO GROUT, BUT IN NARROW JOINTS SANDED GROUT DOES NOT PACK AS WELL AS UN-SANDED GROUT.) TO HIDE SMALL DIFFERENCES IN THE WIDTH OF GROUT LINES ON YOUR COUNTERS, CHOOSE A GROUT COLOR THAT MATCHES YOUR GRANITE. WHERE TILE MEETS A DIFFERENT SURFACE, SUCH AS THE WOOD TRIM ON THIS ISLAND, USE SANDED CAULK IN THE JOINTS.

19 Apply the thinset to the backerboard as you did to the counter underlayment, stopping at the inner grout lines you marked in Step 11. Again, the ridges should be two-thirds the depth of the notches on your trowel.

20 Place a corner tile along the inner grout lines. Set the tile straight down, parallel to the surface. Place spacers at each corner.

21 Place the next tile, aligning it with the first tile and fitting it snugly against the spacers. Check the surface with a carpenter's level and adjust the tiles if necessary.

22 Continue laying the tiles in your prearranged pattern, adding spacers between tiles. Keep checking your work with a level. Allow the thinset to dry for 24 hours.

NOTE: Tiles come with a tiny bevel on the edges. When you cut tiles, the cut edges won't have bevels. As a result, the grout lines between cut tiles will appear narrower than those between uncut tiles, even though you're using the same-size spacers.

Adding the Trim

23 Refinish the trim, sanding it and then resealing it with several coats of varathane on all edges to protect it from moisture.

24 Reattach the trim. If it was originally secured with finishing nails, nail through the existing holes.

25 Tape off the trim with blue tape to protect it before you apply the grout.

Grouting the Tile

26 Mix the grout according to the manufacturer's instructions. (Use sanded caulk instead of regular grout on those edges where tile meets wood trim.) Holding the float at a slight angle, as shown, push the grout between the tiles, working in all directions and packing the grout as firmly as possible.

27 As soon as a haze starts to form, sponge the tile with a wrung-out, nearly dry sponge. (A wet sponge will weaken the grout.) Keep a bucket of fresh water handy to rinse the sponge often. Be sure to wear gloves because grout is alkaline and will irritate your skin.

28 After curing the grout for 24 hours, carefully seal the tile and the grout according to the manufacturer's instructions.

Tiling Around an Outlet

Remove the outlet cover or switch plate. Carefully measure around the opening to determine the necessary dimensions of the tile pieces you must cut. (The pieces, plus the opening, should add up to the dimensions of one tile.) SEE RIGHT. **Cut the tile pieces.**

Working on a slick surface, such as a sheet of plastic, apply silicone sealant to the cut edges of the tile pieces. SEE RIGHT. **(The silicone holds the pieces together long enough for you to put them up as one unit; the thinset secures them.)**

Treat the unit as one tile and apply it to the wall. SEE BELOW.

MATERIALS

Kraft paper or drop cloth

Clean, brown paper bags

Paintbrushes to apply wallpaper paste and polyurethane

Premixed, heavy-duty wallpaper paste (the smallest tub will suffice)

Clean, soft rags

Metal straightedge

Utility knife

Universal tints, in black and burnt umber, available at home centers and paint stores

4 ounces of water-based glazing medium

Clear plastic wrap

Water-based, low-luster polyurethane

Tinted furniture finish wax, in antique pine, available through woodworking catalogs

MAKEOVER MAGIC

Paper Bag Island

THE LOWLY BROWN PAPER BAG makes an innovative wallpaper for the sides of the island. The process is more like decoupage than traditional wallpapering: you tear the bags into irregular shapes, crumple them, then paste them over the island to create a new surface that's rich in both actual and visual texture. When glazed, sealed, and waxed, it resembles worn leather. Note that the wax used is tinted furniture finish wax, which is different from furniture cleaning wax.

TIP

BROWN PAPER BAGS VARY

IN COLOR FROM STORE TO

STORE. IT'S BEST TO GATHER

BAGS FROM THE SAME PLACE;

IF YOU USE BAGS FROM

DIFFERENT SOURCES, MIX

THE TORN PIECES SO ANY

COLOR VARIATIONS ARE

EVENLY DISTRIBUTED OVER

THE ISLAND.

Preparing the Island

1 Lay down floor protection. Remove any switch plates or outlet covers from the island; wash them and the sides of the island with mild soap and water.

Papering the Sides

2 Tear the bags into pieces, ripping off the upper "pinked" edges and discarding them. Do not use the printed sections of the bags; the color may bleed through the paper.

3 Crumple the pieces. Unfold one piece and brush wallpaper paste onto one side.

4 Place the first piece on the island, anywhere away from a corner. Smooth the piece firmly with your hands.

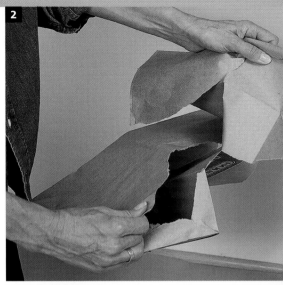

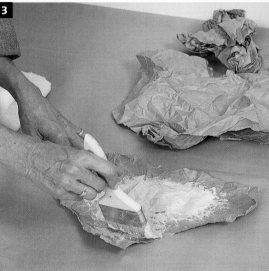

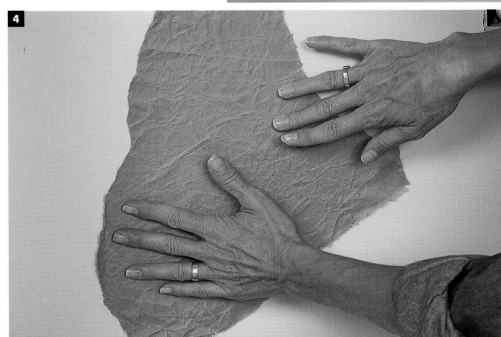

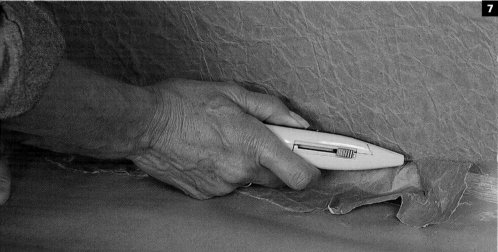

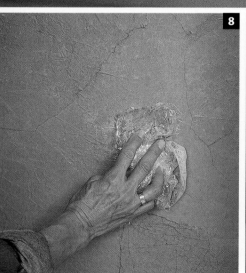

5 With a damp rag, gently wipe off the excess paste from the piece. Don't rub it more than necessary or the paper will begin to disintegrate.

6 Continue pasting pieces to the island surface, overlapping the edges and wiping the excess paste. Don't overlap more than necessary or the surface may appear irregular. Wrap pieces around corners and extend pieces beyond the top and bottom edges. (You'll trim the excess paper in the next step.) At electrical outlets, continue the pieces just far enough for the outlet covers to hide the edges of the paper. Cover the entire surface with paper pieces; allow the wall to dry for several hours.

7 Once the pieces have dried to the touch, trim off the excess paper at the upper and lower edges of the island using the metal straightedge and the utility knife.

Tinting and Sealing the Surface

8 Add a few drops of each universal tint to the glazing medium. Using a crumpled-up piece of clear plastic wrap, apply the glazing medium to the paper surface with a dabbing motion. Allow the wall to dry for several hours. Reserve the remaining tint-glaze mixture for the outlet covers (see Step 12).

9 Brush the surface with the polyurethane. Allow the wall to dry overnight.

Waxing the Surface

10 Using a soft, dry rag, apply furniture finish wax to the surface in a circular motion. Allow it to dry a few minutes; buff with a clean rag.

11 If your island has painted legs, you may wax them as well.

Papering Outlet Covers and Switch Plates

12 Tear small pieces of paper and use wallpaper paste to apply them to the front of any outlet covers or switch plates, covering the openings and wrapping the edges around to the back. Smooth the paper with your fingers. Allow to dry for several hours. Apply tinted glaze as in Step 8.

13 With the outlet cover or switch plate facedown, use the utility knife to make several slits through the paper covering the openings, working from the edge to the center. Fold the paper to the back of the cover or plate, trim the excess, and adhere the paper with wallpaper paste. Allow to dry for several hours.

14 Brush the outlet cover or switch plate with polyurethane and allow it to dry overnight. Wax as in Step 10.

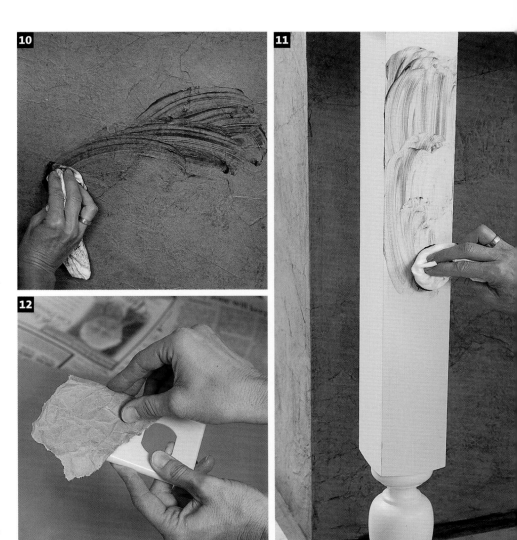

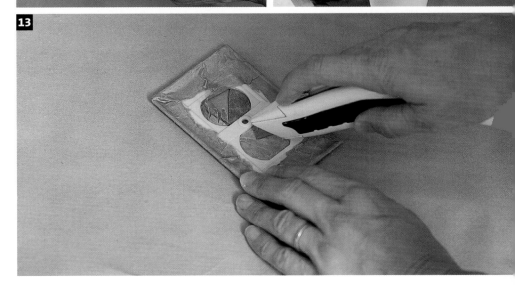

MATERIALS

Craft knife

¼-inch foam-core board, slightly larger than the door cutout

Spiral saw

Spackling compound

100-grit sandpaper

Latex primer

Paintbrushes

Latex paint in three colors (see tip at right)

Paint-crackling medium

Light-duty kitchen scrubber sponge

Sharp tools (paint key, hammer, and hand drill) to distress the surface

Tinted furniture finish wax, in antique pine, available through wood-working catalogs

½-inch wire mesh

Bronze spray paint

Permanent marker

Tin snips

Staple gun

Fabric for panels*

Thread

18-gauge picture-framing wire**

Small wood screws

Scissors

MAKEOVER MAGIC

Antiqued Hutch

A DATED MAPLE HUTCH takes on a European country look with a decorative paint finish and door cutouts that accommodate wire-mesh insets and gathered fabric panels. Scrubbing the painted surface with a kitchen scrubber sponge reveals layers of coral and yellow paint underneath a top coat of green. Crackling medium on the inside back enhances the Old World look. You can use almost any size wire mesh for the doors, depending on the effect you want.

*See Step 10 to determine yardage. **See Step 12 to determine length.*

TIP

FOR PAINT COLORS, FIRST
CHOOSE THE OVERALL COLOR
(THE TOP COAT) FOR THE
HUTCH. FOR THE TWO UNDER-
COATS SELECT COLORS THAT
PICK UP HUES IN THE SCHEME;
ON THIS HUTCH YELLOW
ECHOES THE WALL COLOR,
AND CORAL IS ONE OF THE
COLORS IN THE VALANCE
FABRIC. BE SURE THE THREE
COLORS ARE SIMILAR IN
INTENSITY (BRIGHTNESS OR
DULLNESS) AND VALUE
(LIGHTNESS OR DARKNESS).

Cutting Out the Doors

1 Remove all the doors from the hutch. Save the hardware for remounting the doors later. For the doors that will have wire-mesh insets, use a craft knife to cut a foam-core template that's ¼ inch smaller all around than the panel to be cut out. You'll use this template to support the spiral saw.

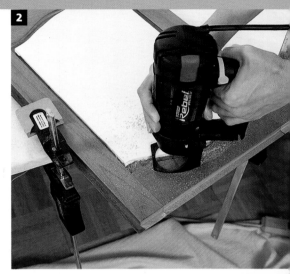

2 With the template resting on the door panel, cut out each panel flush with the inner edges of the door frame. Fill any nicks in the edges with spackling compound; let the compound dry, then sand the edges smooth.

Painting the Hutch and Doors

3 Where doors will not be rein-stalled, fill screw holes with spackle. Lightly sand and prime the hutch, shelves, and door frames. Apply one coat of each color of latex paint, finishing with the desired hutch color. Let the paint dry after each coat. Apply the crackling medium to the back of the shelves, following the manufacturer's instructions.

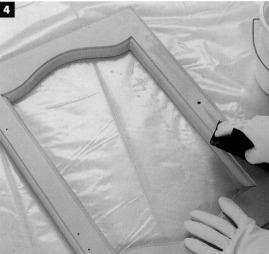

4 Scrub the hutch, shelves, and door frames with the kitchen scrubber sponge.

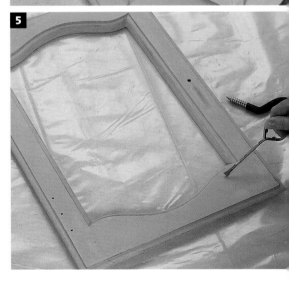

5 Distress the hutch, shelves, and door frames with the sharp tools.

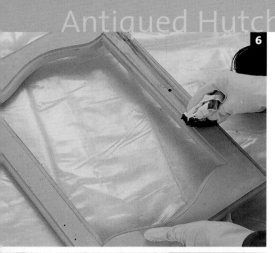

6 Wax the hutch, shelves, door frames, and backs of shelves with the tinted furniture finish wax. Allow to dry; buff with a rag.

Attaching the Wire Mesh

7 Spray-paint both sides of the wire mesh. Allow one side to dry before painting the other.

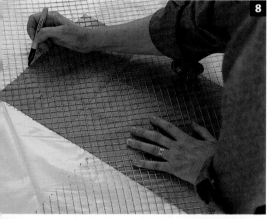

8 Make a paper pattern 1 inch larger all around than the door cutout. Lay the wire mesh, on the diagonal, over the pattern and outline the pattern with a permanent marker. Repeat to outline all mesh insets. Cut out with tin snips.

9 Trim the corners of the wire. Using the staple gun, staple the mesh to the backs of the door frames every 3 inches.

Adding the Fabric Panels

10 For each mesh door you'll need one piece of fabric. The width should be two times the width of the door cutout. The length should equal the length of the cutout plus 4 inches total for the top and bottom rod pockets, plus whatever extra length you need to position the rod pockets so they won't show from the front.

11 Working on the wrong side of one fabric piece, machine-stitch a narrow hem at each side edge. At the top and bottom of the panel,

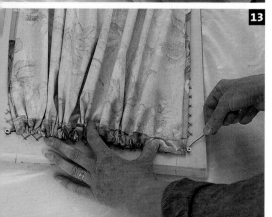

fold in 2 inches and press. Unfold and turn the raw edge in to meet the pressed fold; refold, pin, and stitch close to the inside fold to make each rod pocket. Repeat on the other fabric piece or pieces.

12 Cut pieces of picture-framing wire twice as long as each door cutout is wide, plus about 8 inches; cut the pieces in half. These wires will be inserted in the top and bottom rod pockets to hold the fabric panels in place.

13 Measure the length of the fabric panels. Using this measurement, mark positions on the backs of the doors for the screws that will hold the wires. Insert the top two screws. Thread a piece of wire through the top rod pocket. Wrap the ends of the wire tightly around the screws; snip the ends.

14 Thread the second piece of wire through the bottom rod pocket. Before you insert the bottom two screws, check to see that when the wire is attached the fabric panel will be taut lengthwise. If it won't, lower the screw marks slightly; insert the screws. Wrap the ends of the wire tightly around the screws; snip the ends close to the screws.

Finishing the Hutch

15 Remount the doors on the hutch using the original hardware.

MATERIALS

Latex primer

Paint roller

Foam roller covers

Paint tray and two
disposable tray liners

2-inch paintbrush

¾-inch MDF, cut to size
(see the tip on page 74)

2-inch molding, enough
to frame the edges
of the MDF, plus at least
6 inches on each piece

Miter box with
backsaw

Latex paint for
molding

Latex
blackboard paint

Wood glue

Ten all-purpose clamps

Blue painter's tape

Tinted furniture finish
wax, in antique pine,
available through wood-
working catalogs

Soft rag

L-brackets with screws
(see Step 9)

IN A WEEKEND

Blackboard Message Center

IN MANY OPEN KITCHENS, one side of the refrigerator is in plain view,
giving even the best-decorated rooms an unfinished look. An attractive
and practical solution is to cover the exposed side with a full-length message center made of medium-density fiberboard (MDF) that's been coated
with blackboard paint and trimmed with decorative molding. This molding was painted to match the hutch (see page 70) and the phone table (see
page 81), distributing the color around the room.

FINISHED SIZE 29 by 69 inches

T I P

TAILOR YOUR MESSAGE
CENTER TO YOUR REFRIGERA-
TOR'S SIZE. FOR THE WIDTH,
MEASURE FROM THE BASE-
BOARD AT THE WALL TO THE
POINT WHERE THE DOORS
BEGIN. (THE DOORS MUST BE
FREE TO SWING OPEN.) FOR
THE LENGTH, MEASURE FROM
THE FLOOR TO JUST BELOW
THE OVERHEAD CABINETS.
(AN L-BRACKET WILL SECURE
THE TOP OF THE MDF TO THE
BOTTOM OF THE CABINETS.)
IF YOU DON'T HAVE OVERHEAD
CABINETS, MEASURE TO THE
TOP OF THE REFRIGERATOR
AND PLAN TO SECURE THE
BOARD TO THE WALL.

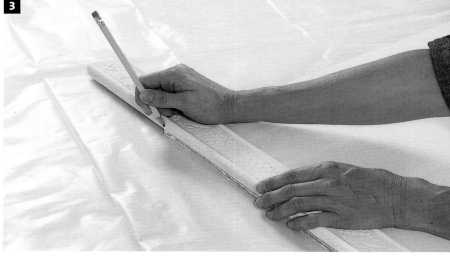

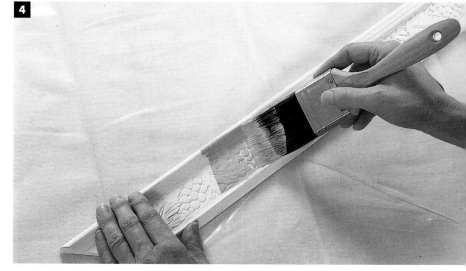

1 Prime the MDF and the molding. (Use the roller and a foam cover on the MDF and the brush on the molding.)

2 Using the miter box, make the first 45-degree-angle cut on one molding piece.

3 Hold the just-cut piece of molding against the corresponding edge of the MDF and mark the point for the second miter cut; make the cut. Cut the remaining three pieces of molding in the same way.

4 Paint the molding pieces with latex paint.

5 Using the paint roller with a foam roller cover, paint the MDF with the blackboard paint. Allow the paint to dry; apply two more coats.

6 Paint the edges of the MDF piece with the same color latex paint you used on the molding.

7 Apply wood glue to the back of each molding piece. (If you want to be able to slip papers and pictures under the molding, don't apply glue to the inside edges.) Set each piece in place and secure with the all-purpose clamps, protecting the molding with soft cloths if necessary. Allow the glue to dry.

8 Mask the edges of the blackboard surface with painter's tape as shown. Apply tinted wax to the molding with a soft rag, wiping off the excess and buffing the surface.

9 If you have overhead cabinets, screw one L-bracket to the underside of the cabinets at the front edge. Position the blackboard against the baseboard, with its lower edge approximately 1 inch forward so the board leans back slightly. Screw the other end of the L-bracket to the back of the board. Gently kick the lower edge of the board in for a snug fit. If you don't have overhead cabinets, attach the blackboard to the wall using two L-brackets, one at the top and one at the bottom.

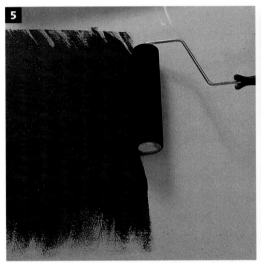

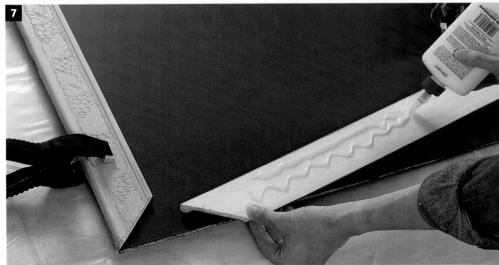

MATERIALS

Two 18-inch
chenille pillows

1⅛ yards of
muslin to back the
pillows

2¼ yards of
brush fringe,
1¾ inches wide

⅝ yard of bonded
quilt batting,
90 inches wide

Fabric scissors

Pins

Thread to blend

DO IT TODAY

Petite Pillows

SMALL CHENILLE PILLOWS edged with brush fringe offer a bit of plush comfort for those seated at the table. Yardage like this would be pricey, but taking apart two 18-inch pillows from a discount department store made it possible to create four half-size pillows and dress them up fairly inexpensively. The original pillows for this project were made from 36-inch-long rectangles folded in half.

FINISHED SIZE four pillows, each approximately 9 by 18 inches

TIP

IF EACH PURCHASED

PILLOW IS MADE FROM

TWO SQUARES OF CHE-

NILLE, BACK EACH SQUARE

WITH A SAME-SIZE MUSLIN

PIECE; PIN THE LAYERS

AT THE EDGES AND

ZIGZAG AROUND THEM.

THEN SKIP TO STEP 5.

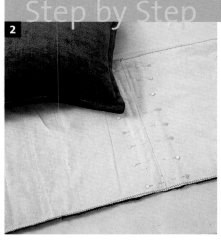

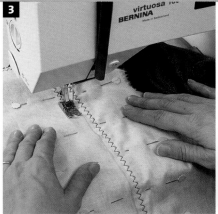

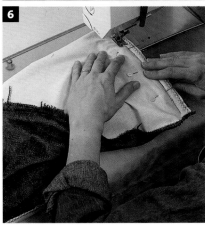

1 Take each pillow apart, creating two chenille rectangles. Set aside the filling. Cut two rectangles of muslin, each the size of a chenille rectangle.

2 Mark a center line vertically on each muslin rectangle. Pin each rectangle, marked side up, to the wrong side of a pillow piece; zigzag around the edges. Also pin on either side of the center line through both layers.

3 Zigzag on either side of the center line as close as possible to the line without overlapping the stitching.

4 Cut each chenille-and-muslin piece on the line, creating two squares, each approximately 18 by 18 inches. You should now have four squares.

5 Cut eight pieces of fringe, each equal in length to one-half the measurement of the chenille-and-muslin square, less 1/2 inch. On opposite sides of each square, position a fringe piece 1/2 inch from the upper edge. Also set it in from the side edges so that a 1/2-inch seam will reveal the maximum of fringe, but not any of the fringe edging, when the pillow is turned right side out. Baste the fringe to the square.

6 Fold each square in half horizontally; pin. (Inside, each piece of fringe should stop at the fold.) Stitch on the short edges through all layers, using a 1/2-inch seam allowance. Turn right side out.

7 To make pillow forms, cut four squares of batting, each 18 by 18 inches. Fold each in half, pin, and stitch across one short edge and along the long edge, using a 1/2-inch seam allowance. Stuff with the filling. Stitch the open end closed by machine.

8 Insert the pillow forms into the chenille covers. Turn in the long raw edges 1/2 inch and slipstitch closed.

Transforming
Touches

Secondary Seating

RIGHT: **Custard-and-cream-colored chenille brightens the chairs and ottoman and resonates with the warm, textured walls.**

Anything-but-Ordinary Hardware

LEFT: **A continuous valance hangs from a copper rod made of standard 1-inch tubing, elbows, and end caps. The copper pieces were spray-painted black, scrubbed with steel wool, then sponge-painted green, followed by silver.**

Bay View

RIGHT: **Before, miniprint wallpaper and tapered valances dated the cozy bay seating area opposite the kitchen. Rattan chairs still looked fresh, but the country-style hutch was a prime candidate for change.** LEFT: **After, frescolike walls make a warm backdrop for the reinvented hutch, which now sits angled in the corner to give the room a more open look. The unfinished pine table was chosen for its light tone and graceful shape.**

New Old Glass

Decorative glass with a subtle antique pattern veils the view through the cabinet doors. Glass suppliers will remove existing glass, cut the new pieces, and fit them into your doors.

Phone Table

LEFT: **A miniature cabinet made of MDF scraps and a discarded hutch door and hardware provides a special place, off the counter, for the phone and other necessities. Narrow beaded molding trims the front edges.**

Topiary Ivy

BELOW: **Tendrils of needlepoint ivy wrap around a circular wire frame fashioned from a plain coat hanger. (The hook portion of the hanger was straightened and stuck into the soil.)**

Handsome Handles

ABOVE: **Brushed-nickel bin pulls update the cabinet drawers and harmonize with other new hardware.**

Display Shelf

ABOVE: **The homeowner turned a small glass shelf, a yard-sale find, into a place to display a ginger jar. The shelf sits, unattached, on the edges of the backsplash tile.**

Island Edging

ABOVE: **Resin trim finished to look like metal completes the edges of the island in style and repeats fruit-and-leaf motifs that appear elsewhere in the scheme. The trim is available through tile suppliers and is attached with thinset, a tile adhesive.**

Fabric Trim

RIGHT: **A fabric sleeve over the chandelier cord softens and downplays a plain electrical cord. Bias-cut strips of plaid fabric, their edges left raw, were glued around the lower edges of the shades for a custom look.**

Dishwasher Update

STEP ONE Loosen the screws on the sides of the dishwasher door and the kickplate. Slide out the old skins and the cardboard. Save the cardboard.

STEP TWO Take the skins to a sheet-metal supplier to have replacements cut. When you pick up the new skins, check them against your old ones to make sure they are precisely the same size. (Small differences can make it difficult to install the new skins.)

STEP THREE Slide in the original cardboard, followed by the new skins.

STEP FOUR Tighten the screws on the sides of the door and kickplate.

ABOVE: Replacement "skins" make an old dishwasher look nearly new. A sheet-metal supplier can cut 24-gauge, brushed stainless-steel pieces like the ones shown here.

Sea Change

WITH A LITTLE PAINT, beadboard, fabric, and hardware, this kitchen went from pleasant and unfinished to positively shipshape. Walls the color of coastal waters form the backdrop for the pristine white cabinetry and beadboard island. Deeper blue cabinet inserts and grommeted valances—along with high-gloss table and counter surfaces—contribute to the nautical look. In this clean, spare space, everyone's gaze goes first to the black-and-white photo gallery (see page 95) that fills what was once a blank wall in the dining area with a visual record of this family's active life.

Recently remodeled, the space had everything going for it—great light, an open atmosphere, and an efficient floor plan.

Cabinet Inserts

INSERTS MADE OF FOAM-CORE BOARD, painted with latex paint and trimmed to fit, are an easy alternative to painting the inside of your cabinets. If the shelf placement is the same in each cabinet, you'll need to cut only a few patterns; these cabinets required just four. When choosing paint, keep in mind that any color will look darker inside cabinets. If you want to lighten the interior, err on the side of a brighter, lighter color.

Measure your cabinets to determine how many sheets you will need. Buy an extra sheet to allow for cutting errors.

MATERIALS

Steel tape measure

Tracing paper

Sheets of ¼-inch foam-core board, available at art supply and office supply stores*

Paint roller with foam roller cover

Latex paint

Paint tray with disposable liner

Metal straightedge

Craft knife

Rotary cutting mat

TIP

PAINT THE OTHER SIDE OF
THE FOAM-CORE BOARD A
DIFFERENT COLOR SO YOU
CAN REVERSE THE INSERTS
FOR A SEASONAL CHANGE.

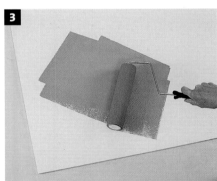

Step by Step

1 Using the steel tape, roughly measure each area at the inside back of the cabinets from shelf to shelf and side to side.

2 For each different-size area, cut a piece of tracing paper slightly larger than the dimensions. By trial and error, fold the pieces of paper into patterns that fit perfectly against the cabinet back. Subtract ⅛ inch from the height and width of each paper pattern (¹⁄₁₆ inch on each edge) to arrive at the cut size of each insert. Do not cut the foam-core board yet.

3 Using the paint roller with foam roller cover, paint one side of each foam-core sheet. Allow the paint to dry. Flip the board over and paint the other side. (You need to paint both sides of the board to keep it from warping.)

4 Do a little math to determine how to cut the inserts most efficiently from the sheets of foam-core board. Measure each paper pattern; mark the dimensions on the board for as many pieces as you need. Cut out the inserts using the metal straightedge, craft knife, and cutting mat.

5 Remove the shelves. Working from the bottom up, place each insert against the back of the cabinet; replace the shelf just above it. If the insert is too snug, remove it and trim slightly; if it's too small, cut another piece.

MATERIALS

Steel tape measure

Fabric scissors

White cotton or
cotton-linen fabric,
54 or 60 inches wide*

White drapery lining,
48 inches or wider*

Carpenter's square

6- by 24-inch rotary
ruler or yardstick

¼-inch blue painter's
tape

Plastic drop cloth

Latex paint or opaque
acrylic craft paint in
four colors

Textile medium
(see Step 8)

Small, flat paintbrush

Pins

White thread

Grommet set and
¾-inch grommets
(number depends on
valance width; see
Step 16)

Wood scrap

Hammer

½-inch curtain rod with
brackets

*See Step 1 for yardage.

NOTE: Do not prewash
the fabrics.

SEWING WORKSHOP

Painted Valance

CRISP PAINTED STRIPES and shiny grommets turn plain white fabric into a jaunty valance. The light and dark blue latex paints were left over from the walls and the cabinet inserts (see page 86); pale yellow and taupe were added to complete the palette. Grommets this large—¾ inch in diameter—can be hard to come by; check out suppliers of boating materials and marine equipment.

FINISHED SIZE 15 inches long

Determining the Yardage

1 For each valance, measure the width of the window opening; add the extensions (the distance the rod will extend beyond the window) and the returns (the distance the rod projects from the wall). Multiply this number by 1¼. Divide by 36 to determine the yardage for the face fabric and for the lining. If you're making two valances, buy yardage for the longer one (see the tip at left).

Painting the Face Fabric

2 Cut the face fabric in half lengthwise. (For 54-inch fabric, each half will be 27 inches wide.) The following instructions are for one valance, made from one half. Repeat Steps 3 through 21 to make a second valance from the other half.

3 Carefully trim off the selvage from the face fabric. Lightly press the fabric and lay it right side up on your work surface.

4 On a 4- by 6-inch index card or a piece of stiff paper, draw a template for the stripe pattern, using the dimensions shown below. The sequence repeats itself at the stripe labeled "First stripe repeat." (After you mark the stripe pattern on your fabric, you'll apply tape along the ¼-inch lines.)

4

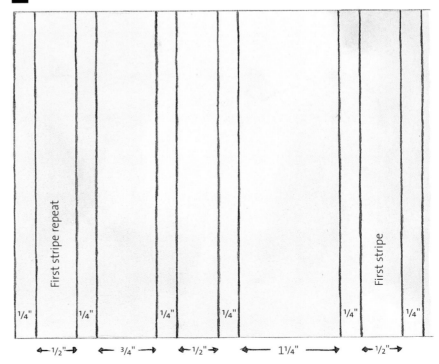

5

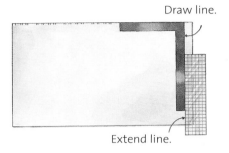

Draw line.

Extend line.

5 Using the template, mark the pattern on the upper edge (a long edge) of the fabric. Next, lay the carpenter's square so its short arm is aligned with the upper edge and its long arm is aligned with the first mark. Draw a line along the edge of the long arm. Using a rotary ruler or yardstick, extend the line to the opposite long edge of the fabric. Use the template to mark the remainder of the lower edge. Make

sure the marks align precisely up and down, or your stripes will "lean" in one direction.

6 Tape the fabric at the ¼-inch marks, working from one end. Extend the tape beyond the fabric edges, as shown at right, but do not stretch it. With your fingers, press firmly on the edges of the tape to prevent paint from seeping underneath.

7 Identify the color of each stripe to be painted with letters at the upper edge; for example, Y for yellow, LB for light blue. Cover your work surface with the plastic drop cloth in preparation for painting.

8 For latex paint, mix the paint and the textile medium in a 1:1 ratio. For opaque acrylic craft paint, follow the directions on the textile medium container. Paint the stripes, working with one color at a time. Allow the paint to dry.

9 Remove the tape.

Stitching the Valance

10 Measure, mark, and trim the long edges of the painted fabric so the stripes measure 24 inches up and down.

11 Trim the selvage on the lining. Measure, mark, and cut the lining so it measures 8 inches up and down.

6

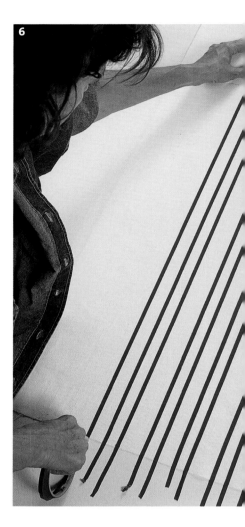

8

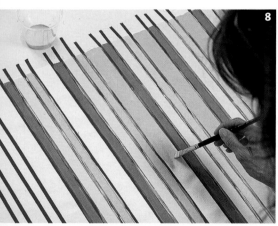

9

TIP

SHIFT THE FABRIC AS NEEDED TO CONTINUE PAINTING. BUT BEFORE YOU MOVE A "FRESH" AREA OF FABRIC INTO POSITION, WIPE UP ANY WET PAINT THAT HAS SEEPED THROUGH THE FABRIC ONTO YOUR WORK SURFACE.

12 With the lining against the painted side of the face fabric and aligned with one long raw edge, stitch the two pieces using a ½-inch seam allowance, as shown. Using a dry iron set on "polyester," press the seam allowances toward the lining.

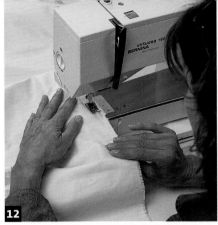

13 Right sides together, stitch the other long edges of the painted fabric and the lining, forming a tube; press the seam allowances toward the lining. Turn the tube right side out.

14 Smooth and adjust the tube to create a 3½-inch heading along one edge and a 4½-inch hem on the other edge. Press.

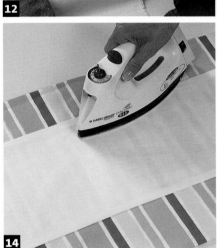

15 At each end of the valance, turn in the raw edges ½ inch and pin. Slipstitch the ends closed.

Setting the Grommets

16 Measure the width of the valance (the long measurement); subtract 1½ inches from each end (the distance from the end of the valance to the center of the outer grommet). Divide the remainder by 8 (the spacing, in inches, between grommets on this valance) to arrive at the number of spaces on your valance. In all likelihood, this number will include a fraction. Adjust the spacing between grommets until you come up with a whole number of spaces. You'll need one more grommet than spaces.

17 With the valance right side up, measure and mark a center point for a grommet 1½ inches from the upper and the side edges at each end.

18 Starting from one of the center points marked in the previous step and using the space size you determined in Step 16, measure and lightly mark center points for the grommets across the width of the valance.

19 Place a piece of scrap wood underneath the first grommet mark. Position the grommet cutter over the mark; hit firmly with a hammer. Repeat to cut the remaining grommets.

20 Set each grommet.

21 Install the curtain-rod brackets following the manufacturer's instructions. Thread the valance onto the rod and attach it to the brackets. If the valance is too full, take it down and trim it so the second grommet from the end becomes the end grommet. Turn in the raw edges and slipstitch closed. (Be sure to maintain the 1½ inches from the grommet center to the side edge.)

MATERIALS

4- by 8-foot sheets of ¼-inch MDF beadboard, enough to cover the back and sides of the island (see Step 1)

Steel tape measure

Circular saw

Spiral saw for cutting out openings

Masking tape/paper dispenser, available at paint stores

Latex primer

100-grit sandpaper

White latex paint

Paint tray with disposable liner

2-inch paintbrush

Wood glue

Electric brad nailer with ½-inch nails

Paintable wood putty

IN A WEEKEND

Beadboard Island

THE HOMEOWNERS made this island using stock cabinets (one 2 feet long, the other 3 feet long) to match their fitted cabinets, all from a home center. To give it a custom look, they added MDF beadboard to the backs and sides of the stock components. One edge of each beadboard sheet needs to be mitered at a cabinet shop, home center, or lumberyard; you can measure and cut the other edges at home.

TIP

YOU HAVE SEVERAL OPTIONS
FOR FINISHING THE MDF
BEADBOARD AT THE LOWER
EDGES. IF THE EDGE IS
SMOOTH, YOU CAN LEAVE IT
AS IS. FOR A MORE FINISHED
LOOK, PRIME, PAINT, AND
INSTALL SHOE BASEBOARD
(SHOWN ABOVE), MITERING
THE CORNERS; THIS IS A
GOOD CHOICE NO MATTER
WHAT YOUR FLOORING. IF
YOUR FLOORS ARE VINYL OR
TILE, CONSIDER INSTEAD
RUNNING A BEAD OF SILICONE
ACRYLIC CAULK AT THE
FLOOR LINE.

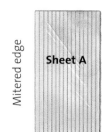

Step by Step

Cutting the Pieces

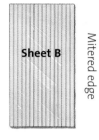

Mitered edge | **Sheet A** | **Sheet B** | Mitered edge

You'll cut pieces 1 and 4 from Sheet A and pieces 2 and 3 from Sheet B.

1 Most islands will require two sheets of MDF beadboard. Have one edge on *each* sheet mitered as follows: With the sheets in the same orientation, miter the *left* edge on the first sheet (label it Sheet A) and the *right* edge on the second sheet (label it Sheet B).

2 Before you start cutting the panels, it's important to understand which edges are mitered on this island. See the illustration below.

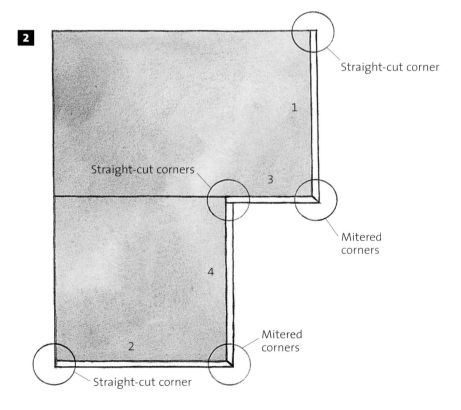

Straight-cut corner

Straight-cut corners

Mitered corners

Mitered corners

Straight-cut corner

93

Gluing the Pieces

6 Apply wood glue to the outer-right side of the island, as shown. Making sure the mitered edge is on the left, adhere the piece to the side of the island.

7 Using the brad nailer and ½-inch nails, nail the beadboard piece to the side of the island around the edges, placing a nail approximately every 6 inches.

8 Next, glue the outer-left piece, with its mitered edge toward the right. Brad-nail in place.

9 Glue the inner-right piece, with its mitered edge to the right, against the mitered edge on the adjoining piece. Brad-nail in place.

10 Glue the inner-left piece, with its mitered edge to the left, against the mitered edge on the adjoining piece. Brad-nail in place.

Finishing the Island

11 Fill the nail holes with wood putty; sand. Apply a second coat of white paint.

3 On Sheet A, measure and mark the outer-right piece of beadboard (labeled 1 on the illustration on the previous page), *making sure the mitered edge is on the left*. Cut the piece using the circular saw; cut out any openings with the spiral saw. Dry-fit the piece against the cabinet as shown. Measure, cut, and dry-fit the remaining pieces, one at a time, in the following order: outer left (2) from Sheet B, inner right (3) from Sheet B, then inner left (4) from Sheet A.

Painting the Pieces

4 Tape paper to the floor to protect the surface.

5 Prime the beadboard pieces; sand lightly with the 100-grit sandpaper. Paint the pieces with the white latex paint.

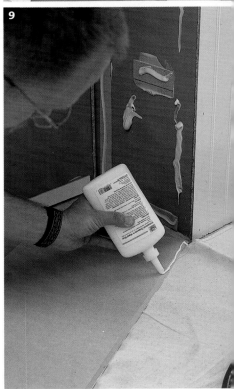

MATERIALS

Color photocopies
(see Steps 1 and 2)

Acrylic pieces
(see Step 1)

¼-inch graph paper
and plain paper, 11 by
17 inches, one sheet of
each per acrylic frame

Blue painter's tape

Hole punch

Felt-tip marker

Wood scraps

Electric drill with
³⁄₁₆- and ³⁄₈-inch
drill bits

Tracing paper

Metal straightedge,
craft knife, and rotary
cutting mat

Antistatic cloth wipes

Repositionable spray
adhesive

Carpenter's level

³⁄₈-inch ribbed plastic
anchors, four per frame

Brake line, available at
automotive parts stores

Tube cutter

Sets of four 2½-, 3-, and
3½-inch #10 screws,
one set per frame

#10 and #12 washers,
four *each* per frame

Screwdriver

IN A WEEKEND

Photo Gallery

THE PICTURES IN THIS GRAPHIC DISPLAY appear to be black and white, but they are actually color photocopies that were made with the color controls turned down. (Color copies, minus the color, have much better resolution than standard black-and-white copies.) The photos are sandwiched between sheets of acrylic and mounted so they stand out from the wall at different distances—1, 1½, and 2 inches—giving the grouping a subtle sense of visual rhythm.

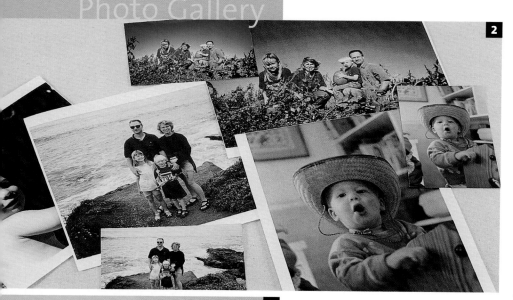

3 On graph paper, draw a layout showing the positions of your framed pictures on the wall. Make sure the different sizes and shapes are distributed evenly across the space; that is, don't put two of the smallest pictures, or two horizontal pictures, side by side.

Preparing the Frames

The directions that follow are for assembling and mounting one photocopy in its acrylic frame. The photocopy measures 7 by 9 inches; the acrylic pieces measure 10 by 12 inches.

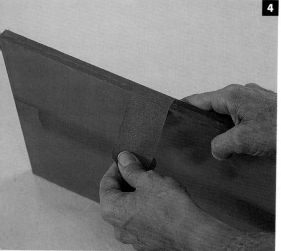

Sizing the Photocopies and the Frames

1 The photocopies in this gallery are three different sizes: 5 by 7, 7 by 9, and 8 by 10 inches. The acrylic frames measure 8 by 10, 10 by 12, and 11 by 13 inches, respectively. Have the acrylic pieces cut at a glass and plastics shop or a framing shop; you'll need two same-size pieces per picture. (If you decide to make your photocopies different sizes than the ones shown in this project, add 1½ inches to each edge to determine the size of the acrylic frames.)

2 Choose your photos and take them to a copy shop to be enlarged and copied onto paper. Make them a little larger than the desired sizes to allow for trimming the edges later. The color controls should be set all the way down.

4 Without removing the protective blue film on the acrylic pieces, tape the pieces together in both directions using blue painter's tape.

5 Cut out a piece of graph paper the same size as the acrylic and mark lines 1½ inches from the edges. Using the hole punch, make a hole in each corner, 1 inch from the edges, for the screw positions. Lay this graph-paper template over the taped-together acrylic and mark the holes using the felt-tip marker. Also mark "top" at the upper edge of the template; set it aside for Step 9.

6 Place a scrap piece of wood under the taped-together acrylic. Using the electric drill with the 3/16-inch bit, drill a hole in each corner at the mark, drilling through

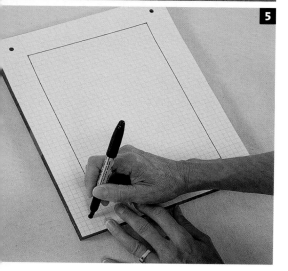

both pieces of acrylic. Run the drill at full speed and do not slow down or stop as you drill each hole. If you slow down, the drill bit may stick.

Cropping the Images

7 Measure and cut a piece of tracing paper the size of the desired image to serve as a cropping pattern. Place the paper over the photocopy and move it around until you're happy with the crop. Draw around the edges, onto the photocopy, to mark the cutting lines.

8 Using the metal straightedge, craft knife, and rotary cutting mat, trim the photocopy on the lines.

Mounting the Images in the Frames

9 Remove the blue tape from the acrylic but do not separate the two pieces. Reposition the graph-paper template on the top piece of acrylic.

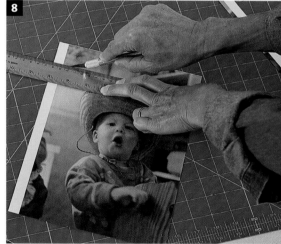

10 Holding the template in place, open the acrylic pieces and lay them flat on your work surface (the template will be underneath one piece). Remove the inside film on each piece of acrylic. Wipe each piece carefully with a separate antistatic cloth.

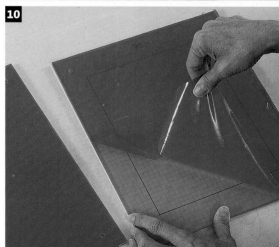

11 Spray the back of the photocopy with repositionable spray adhesive. Looking through the acrylic and using the graph-paper template as a centering guide, position the photo on the acrylic and press lightly.

12 Put the acrylic pieces back together and tape them at the edges to secure until hanging.

Mounting the Pictures on the Wall

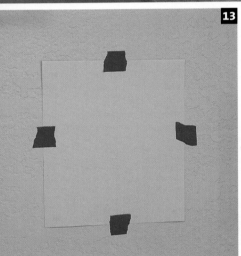

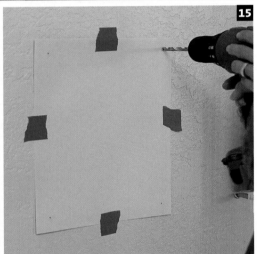

13 Cut a paper template the same size as the acrylic pieces. Referring to your hanging layout (from Step 3), tape the template to the wall.

14 Position the taped-together pieces of acrylic over the template and check the upper edges of the acrylic with a carpenter's level. Mark the paper template through the predrilled holes in the acrylic.

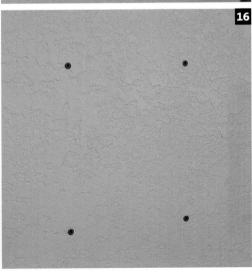

15 Drill through the paper and into the wall at the marks using the 3/8-inch drill bit. Remove the paper.

16 Insert a ribbed plastic anchor into each hole, lightly tapping it with a hammer, if necessary.

17 Measure and mark four 1-inch pieces of brake line for spacers. (Other pictures in the gallery have 1½-inch or 2-inch spacers.) Cut the pieces using the tube cutter.

TIP

TO ACHIEVE AN

UNDULATING EFFECT,

VARY THE SPACER

LENGTHS FROM ONE

FRAME TO THE NEXT.

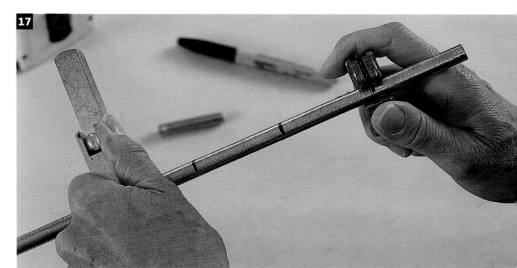

18 Assemble the pieces as follows: Thread a 2½-inch screw through a #10 washer. Working from the front, put the screw with washer through one of the holes in the acrylic, through the brake-line spacer, and through a #12 washer. Repeat on the remaining three corners. With the aid of a helper to hold the screws and washers in place, insert the entire picture unit into the anchors in the wall.

19 Hand-tighten the screws. (If you use a power drill and screw too tightly, you'll crack the acrylic.)

20 Repeat Steps 4 through 19 to assemble and mount additional pictures, using the 3-inch screws with 1½-inch spacers, and the 3½-inch screws with 2-inch spacers.

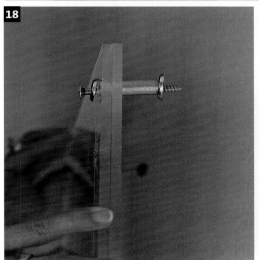

Retro Active

IF KITCHENS COULD SPEAK, this one might say, "It's hip to be square." The checkerboard floor, a signature feature of mid-20th-century kitchens, makes the strongest color-and-design statement, while the bright-colored backsplash tiles, valance, and quilt repeat the square pattern and add visual punch. In a nod to the practicality *and* luxury of the 1950s, metal office chairs get a new coat of paint and sumptuous synthetic suede coverings. Anchoring the color scheme is a freestanding pantry painted bold blue-violet (see page 102). The result? A retro look that's fresh and up-to-date.

This ho-hum galley kitchen needed a boost—on a budget. The main decorating ingredients were paint, tile, and fabric.

Freestanding Pantry

THIS SLIM PANTRY with cross-reeded glass resolves two common issues in a galley kitchen: the need for more storage and the desire to hide the side of the refrigerator. Let a cabinet shop cut the MDF pieces to size (ask for the scraps) and make the pocket holes for the European hinges. A glass supplier can order the glass to fit and install it for you.

FINISHED SIZE 30 inches wide, 12 inches deep, 71¼ inches tall

MATERIALS

Two 4- by 8-foot sheets of ¾-inch MDF, cut as follows:
- Two doors, each 14¹¹/₁₆ by 67⁵/₃₂ inches
- Two sides, each 9¹⁵/₁₆ by 67¼ inches
- One top and bottom, each 10³/₁₆ by 28½ inches
- One crown, 12⅛ by 30⅛ inches
- Five shelves, each 9¹³/₁₆ by 27⅞ inches
- Four cutting guides: two 2⅛ by 10⁷/₁₆ and two 2⅛ by 33½ inches

One 4- by 8-foot sheet of ¼-inch MDF, cut as follows:
- One back, 29⁵/₁₆ by 67⁵/₁₆ inches
- One crown, 12⅛ by 30⅛ inches

Electric drill with ⅜-inch bit, ³/₃₂-inch combination countersink–pilot hole bit, and ¼-inch bit

Jigsaw

Sixteen 1¼-inch #6 wood screws

Router with ½-inch trim bit, ⅜-inch rabbet bit, and ½-inch roundover bit

Wood putty

Sharp chisel

Cross-reeded glass panels

Six full-overlay, European-style hinges with 0mm base plates: three 160- and three 94-degree-angle hinges (see the tip below right)

Twenty-four ¾-inch #6 wood screws

Table saw with dado blade

Carpenter's square

Wood glue

Twelve 1⅝-inch #6 wood screws

Electric brad nailer with 1-inch nails

Small flathead screw

Electric sander with 150- and 220-grit sandpaper discs

Wood clamps

Eight 1¼-inch #8 wood screws

Latex primer and paint

Paint roller with low-nap cover, paintbrush, and paint tray

Four 3-inch chrome feet with screws

Two 4-inch chrome handles with screws

Twenty 5mm or ¼-inch shelf pins

Two 2½-inch #8 wood screws

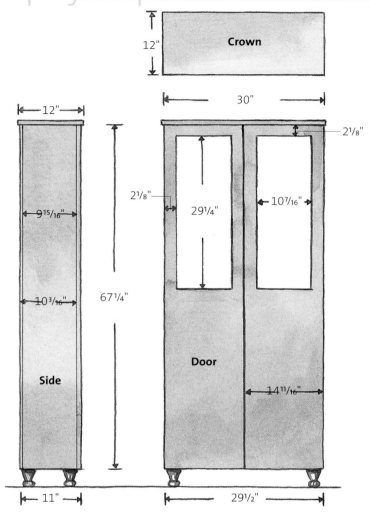

Side, front, and top views illustrate the dimensions of the finished pantry.

EUROPEAN HINGES ALLOW DOORS TO COVER THE ENTIRE FACE OF THE CABINET, WITH NO EXPOSED HARDWARE. A CABINET SHOP SPECIALIZING IN EUROPEAN CONSTRUCTION CAN SUPPLY THE APPROPRIATE HINGES AND DRILL THE NECESSARY HOLES. ASK FOR HINGES WITH "FULL-ADJUSTMENT POTENTIAL."

2

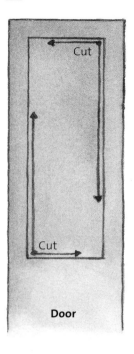

Cut

Cut

Door

3

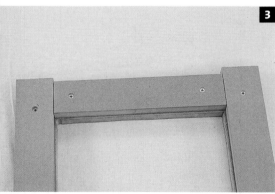

4

5

6

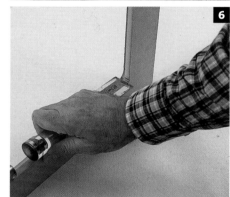

4 Turn the door to the front. Using the router with ½-inch trim bit, trim the door cutout flush with the cutting guides. Turn the door to the back. Remove the cutting guides and putty the screw holes.

5 Repeat Steps 3 and 4 on the other door. *Using the router with the ³/₈-inch rabbet bit adjusted down ³/₈ inch*, trim each cutout to accommodate the glass.

6 Turn the doors to the front. Using the chisel and a hammer, carefully trim the curves on the front to make square corners.

7 Take one of the doors to a glass supplier to have it measured for the two glass inserts. Ask the glass supplier to cut four radii (curves) on each piece of glass to fit the inside curves of each door.

Adding the Hinges

8 Measure and mark the centers for the European hinges 3 inches from the top and bottom of each side piece; allow ⅛ inch from the outside of the door to the edge of each hinge. Measure and mark the center for the middle hinge precisely between the top and bottom marks. Have the cabinet shop cut the holes and, if it has the machine, attach the hinges; see Step 9.

Making the Door Cutouts

1 Using the dimensions shown on the previous page, measure and mark lines on each door for the cutouts. (This side will be the back.) Using the electric drill with ³/₈-inch bit, drill holes in opposite diagonal corners, *just inside the drawn lines.*

2 Starting at the holes and using the jigsaw, cut in either direction, *just inside the drawn lines.* Remove the pieces.

3 Align the four cutting guides with the cutout lines on the back of one door; screw them in place using 1¼-inch #6 screws.

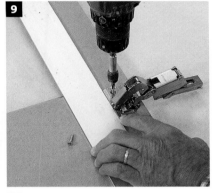

Top

3/4"

Edge of
side piece

1/4"

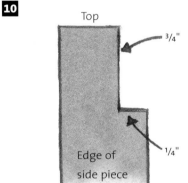

9 Attach the 160-degree-angle hinges on the door that will be toward the center of the room and the 94-degree-angle hinges on the door that will be toward the wall. For each door, start with the bottom hinge in its hole and predrill two screw holes using the 3/32-inch combination countersink–pilot hole bit. Place a straight scrap of wood or MDF up against the inner edge of the hinge to keep it parallel to the door edge. Screw the hinge to the door using 3/4-inch #6 screws. Attach the middle hinge and the top hinge in the same way.

Assembling the Frame

10 Using the table saw with dado blade, notch out the top and bottom edges on the inside of each side piece. (Photo 12 shows this notch.) You may prefer to drill the shelf holes now, before attaching the sides to the top and bottom. See Steps 15 through 18.

11 Hold one side piece and the top piece together so they are perfectly square (check the corner with a carpenter's square). Using the 3/32-inch combination countersink–pilot hole bit, predrill three holes through the side piece and into the top piece.

12 Apply glue to the notch. Adhere the side to the top. Screw the side to the top, using the 1 5/8-inch #6 wood screws. Clean off any excess glue.

13 Repeat to attach the side to the bottom piece. Then attach the other side to the top and bottom pieces to complete the frame.

14 Turn the frame over. Put a bead of glue on the back edges. Center the back on the frame with the aid of a helper. Using the brad nailer and 1-inch nails, attach the back to the sides, top, and bottom, spacing the nails 10 inches apart.

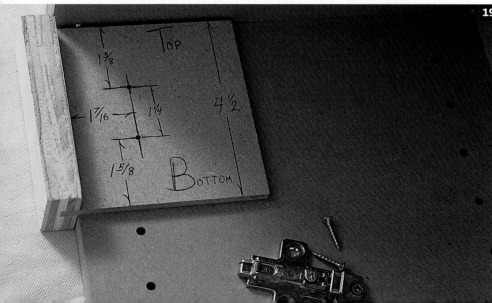

Drilling the Shelf Holes

15 Using a scrap of ¾-inch MDF, make a jig 2½ inches wide and approximately 24 inches long for drilling the shelf holes. Using the ¼-inch bit, drill holes 1¼ inches from the edges, spacing them 1½ inches apart.

16 Drill the holes starting from the bottom of the cabinet. (If you're drilling the holes before you've assembled the frame, measure from the lower edges of the side pieces, starting at the notches.) Choose a hole for your bottommost shelf. On this pantry, the first hole is approximately 9 inches from the bottom, as indicated by "start" written on the jig.

17 Align the jig with a side edge; drill the bottom hole and as many holes above it as are on the jig.

18 Move the jig up so its bottom-most hole is aligned with the last hole you drilled; put a drill bit in the hole to anchor the jig. Continue drilling holes to the point where you want to set the top shelf. Repeat on the other edge and both edges of the other side piece.

Attaching the Base Plates

19 To align the base plates with their corresponding hinges, use scrap MDF or wood to make a jig, including a guide on the front edge.

21

Cut and mark as shown; drill the two holes. At the upper edge of the jig, screw in a small flathead wood screw so that it sticks up $^3/_{32}$ inch. This screw will position the jig (and thus the doors) a little below the top of the pantry, allowing the doors to clear the crown piece. Position the jig flush against the top and front edges of one side. Drill the base plate holes through the jig, into the side, using the $^3/_{32}$-inch combination countersink–pilot hole bit.

20 Place the jig at the bottom of the side piece and drill the holes for the lower base plate.

21 For the middle base plate location, measure and mark the precise midpoint between the upper and lower base plate holes just drilled. Center the jig over the midpoint and drill the holes for the middle base plate.

22 Flip the jig, with the marked side down, to mark the base plate holes on the other side piece. Drill the holes.

23 Screw the base plates into the sides of the frame, using $^3/_4$-inch #6 wood screws.

Finishing the Cabinet

24 With the router and trim bit, trim the back flush with the sides, top, and bottom. Sand with the electric sander, using the 150-grit sanding disc first, followed by the 220-grit disc.

25 Glue the $^1/_4$-inch crown piece to the $^3/_4$-inch crown piece. Clamp and let dry. Using your router with the $^1/_2$-inch roundover bit, finish the front edge, back edge, and side edge that shows (the left side on this pantry; the right side goes against the wall).

26 Lay the crown on the floor with the routed edges facing up. Place the pantry upside down on the crown, flush with the unfinished side, with a $^1/_2$-inch reveal on the other side and on the back, and a $1^1/_4$-inch reveal on the front.

27 Screw the top of the pantry into the crown using eight $1^1/_4$-inch #8 screws, two on each edge.

28 Sand the doors, cabinet, and shelves lightly. Prime with latex primer; paint.

29 Have the glass supplier install the glass.

30 Attach the chrome feet to the underside of the cabinet.

31 Attach the chrome handles to the doors.

32 To mount the doors, snap the hinges into the base plates.

33 Insert the shelf pins at the desired levels and set in the shelves.

34 Using the $2^1/_2$-inch #8 wood screws, secure the pantry to the wall from the inside.

26

½-inch reveal (back edge)

Crown

½-inch reveal (side)

1¼-inch reveal (front edge)

IN A WEEKEND

Vinyl Tile Floor

MATERIALS

Leveling floor compound

Grout tray or similar container

Drywall taping knife

Sanding block with 100-grit sandpaper

Steel tape measure

Tape

Heavy string

Carpenter's square

Chalk line

Vinyl tile, 12 inches square

Knee pads

Gloves

Adhesive comb

Vinyl tile adhesive

Rolling pin

Utility knife

Contour guide

Mineral spirits

Clean rags

Siliconized acrylic caulk and caulking gun (optional)

Buffable acrylic floor polish

IF YOU'RE ON A BUDGET but want a dramatic change underfoot, a vinyl tile floor is the perfect project. You can tile over any subflooring, as long as you use a leveling floor compound first to minimize surface irregularities. The tiles used here are 12 inches square, making it easy to estimate how much you'll need: you buy the number of pieces equal to your kitchen's square footage (add 10 percent to allow for cutting errors). You'll need to buy the tile by the full box; a box contains 45 pieces.

Preparing the Floor

1 Vacuum the subfloor carefully. Mix the leveling floor compound according to the manufacturer's instructions. Using the drywall taping knife, apply the compound to the subfloor over the seams. Allow it to dry.

2 Using the sanding block and 100-grit sandpaper, sand the areas covered by the compound. Vacuum the floor again.

Measuring and Marking the Floor

3 Make a rough sketch of your floor area, noting the dimensions, to help you determine a tiling plan. A good general approach is to center full tiles in the most visible area and work outward, toward the walls. Draw "reference lines" perpendicular to each other through the center of the area; they will help guide tile placement when you transfer the plan to the floor. In this kitchen, full tiles were centered along the length of the galley and the width of the dining area, aligned on either side of the midpoint of the French doors.

TIP

SPREAD THE ADHESIVE AS EVENLY AS POSSIBLE ACROSS THE FLOOR. AS SOON AS YOU APPLY IT, CHECK FOR BLOBS OR BITS OF ADHESIVE ON THE SURFACE; IF YOU FIND ANY, REMOVE THEM WITH A UTILITY KNIFE OR OTHER SHARP TOOL. IMPERFECTIONS IN THE ADHESIVE CAN CAUSE NOTICEABLE BUMPS ON THE TILE ONCE IT'S SET.

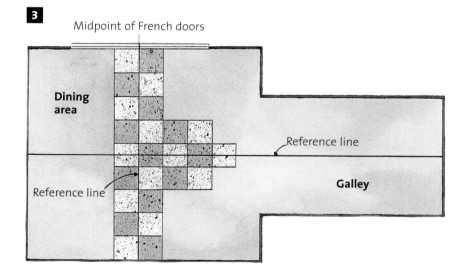

Midpoint of French doors

Dining area

Reference line

Reference line

Galley

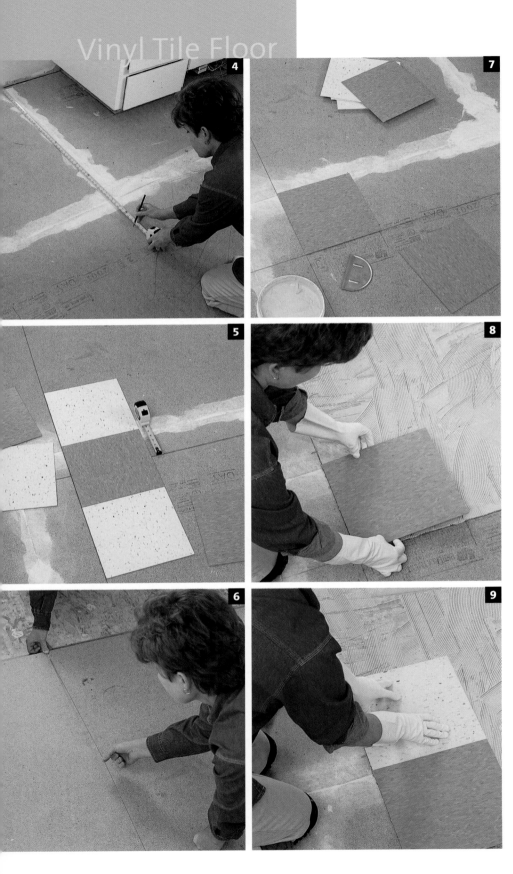

4 Based on your plan, use the steel tape to measure and mark positions for reference lines on the actual subfloor. When marking from a wall, as shown, measure at several points along the wall.

5 Tape heavy string along the reference lines, using a carpenter's square to position the pieces at precise right angles to each other. (For 12-inch tiles to be centered down the length of the galley in this kitchen, they had to be positioned 6 inches to one side of the reference line, as shown.)

6 Once you've determined the position of the center tiles, snap chalk lines as placement guides.

Laying the Tile

7 It's best to set one four-tile section first, starting at one of the right angles formed by the intersecting chalk lines, and work toward the walls and doors in that quadrant. Put on knee pads and gloves. Using the adhesive comb, spread adhesive over the first quadrant; allow it to set up according to the manufacturer's instructions.

8 Set the first tile (green, in this example), lining it up with the chalk lines. Apply light, downward pressure without shifting the tile.

9 Set the second tile (white) next to the first, aligning it with the chalk line and snug against the edge of the first tile; press.

10 Set the third tile (white) and fourth tile (green), as shown, making sure to fit the tiles together snugly.

11 Continue working in one direction until you reach the point where you need to cut tiles. Go over the laid tiles with the rolling pin to set them. Lay the remaining full tiles in the same way.

Cutting Tile to Fit Against a Wall

12 Align the tile to be cut on top of the last full tile near the wall; the illustration at right shows a white tile on top of a green tile.

13 Lay a full tile (green in the illustration) flush with the wall and overlapping the stacked tiles. Using the flush tile as a straightedge, mark the tile to be cut.

14 Cut the marked tile on the line using the carpenter's square and utility knife.

15 Set the cut tile in place to check the fit.

16 Cut the rest of the tiles along the wall and check their fit. Place each tile on top of the row it will

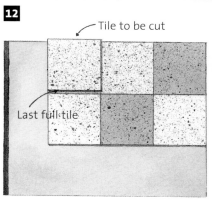

Tile to be cut

Last full tile

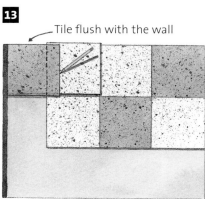

Tile flush with the wall

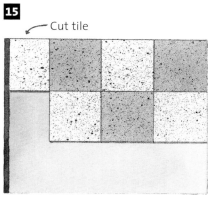

Cut tile

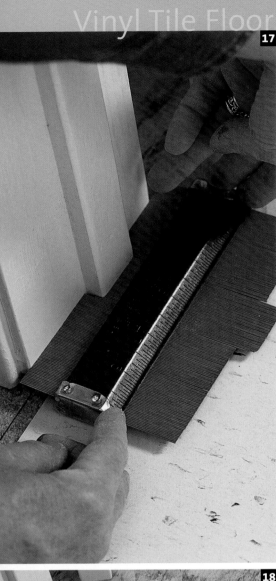

complete. Apply adhesive to the floor and set the tiles in place; go over the tiles with the rolling pin.

Cutting Tile to Fit Around Trim

17 A contour guide allows you to make near-perfect cuts around door trim. Lay the tile to be cut as close to the trim as possible. Position the contour guide on top of the tile and press it against the trim, creating a contour of the shape to be cut out.

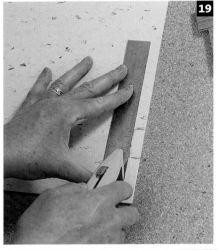

18 Move the tile away from the door trim. Carefully, without disturbing the pins in the guide, set the edge of the guide against the edge of the tile. Mark around the protruding shape.

19 Using the carpenter's square and utility knife, cut out the marked shape.

20 Apply adhesive to the floor and set the tile in place.

Finishing the Tile

21 Clean up any adhesive on the tile surface with mineral spirits and a rag. Lightly wash the tile with mild soap to remove the residue.

22 Run a bead of acrylic caulk along the edge where the tile meets the baseboards, if desired. Apply the acrylic floor polish according to the manufacturer's instructions.

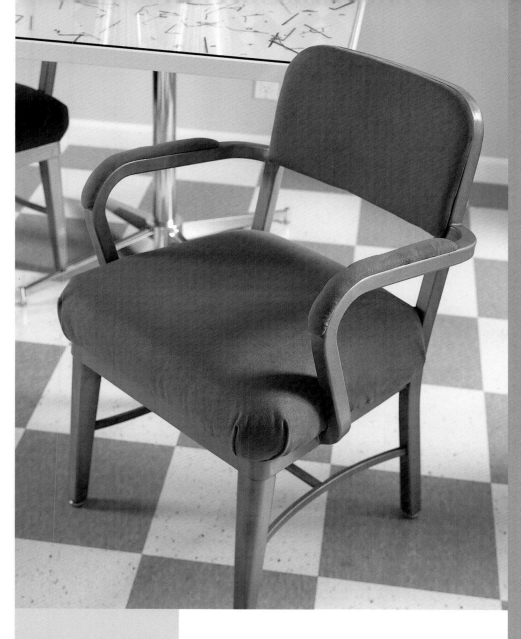

MATERIALS

Office chairs with removable seats, backs, and armrests

Flexible tape measure

Upholstery batting*

Synthetic suede*

¼-inch foam, available at upholstery supply stores*

¾-inch plywood for seat supports**

Felt-tip marker

Electric drill with ⅜-inch bit**

Jigsaw**

Fabric scissors

Staple gun with ⅜-inch staples

Spray adhesive

Hot-glue gun

Trisodium phosphate

Spray paint in hammered-metal finish

Screws (if you must replace existing ones)

*See Steps 1 and 2 for yardage.

**Required only if you replace the seat supports.

IN A WEEKEND

"Suede" Chairs

SYNTHETIC SUEDE and spray paint turned tired-looking office chairs—a real find at $5 each—into plush casual seating. Tailor the steps to suit your chairs; the process is essentially the same, no matter what the components. It's easy to tell the right and wrong sides of synthetic suede: the right side looks and feels like actual suede, while the wrong side is plain.

The following instructions are for one chair; repeat for additional chairs.

Estimating Yardage

1 Take off the chair seat, back, and armrests, reserving the screws if you can reuse them. Measure the pieces and the coverings and make a sketch of them, including dimensions, to take with you when you shop for batting, synthetic suede, and foam.

2 The amount of upholstery batting required depends on the size of the chair seat. You'll need a piece large enough to cover the seat top and sides, plus 2 to 3 inches beyond each lower edge to wrap and staple to the underside. The amount of synthetic suede required depends on the parts to be covered. For the chair seat, allow an extra 4 inches beyond each lower edge to wrap and staple to the underside; for the chair back and armrests, if any, you may be able to use the existing coverings as patterns (see Step 19). The amount of foam required depends on the chair. Here, the inside back and armrests have foam under the suede.

Cutting the Seat Support

3 If the existing seat support is made of wood, skip to Step 6. If it's metal, you'll need to cut a new one out of plywood. Lay the seat support on the plywood and trace around the edges using the felt-tip marker.

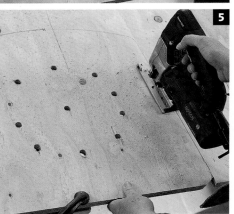

4 Using the electric drill and the ⅜-inch bit, drill venting holes in the plywood.

5 Cut out the seat support using the jigsaw.

Attaching the Batting

6 Lay the chair seat upside down on your work surface. Place the seat support on top.

7 Cut a piece of batting large enough to cover the seat top and sides, plus 2 to 3 inches on all edges. Center the chair seat with plywood seat support on the batting. Bring the batting over the plywood support on opposite sides; gently pull the batting so it's taut. Staple the batting to the plywood, placing three staples at the center on each edge.

8 Staple the batting to the plywood on the adjoining sides, then return to the first sides and staple toward the corners, folding the excess batting around the corners. Finish stapling the adjoining sides. Trim the batting just beyond the staples.

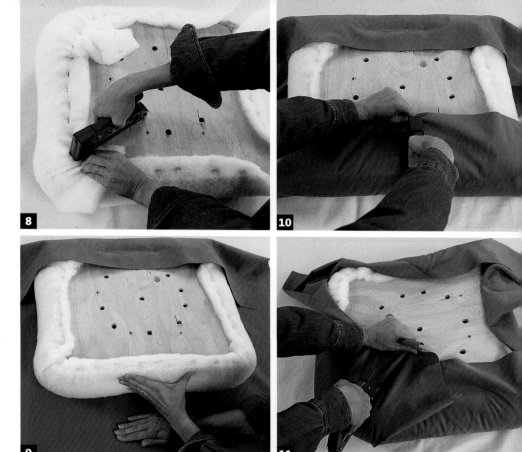

Covering the Seat Cushion

9 Cut a piece of synthetic suede large enough to cover the seat top and sides, plus 4 inches on all edges. Lay the piece on your work surface, *wrong side up*; center the seat upside down on the fabric. Bring the fabric on the far edge to the underside of the seat support, covering the batting staples, and staple the fabric to the plywood as shown. With one hand holding the seat in place, gently pull the near edge of the fabric toward you.

10 Bring the fabric to the underside of the seat support and, holding the fabric taut, staple it to the plywood in the same way.

11 On the free sides, pull the fabric taut and staple it to the plywood. At one corner, pull the fabric in at an angle and staple.

TIP IF YOU RUN YOUR HAND UP AND DOWN THE LENGTH OF SYNTHETIC SUEDE, ITS TEXTURE WILL FEEL SMOOTH IN ONE DIRECTION AND SLIGHTLY RESISTANT IN THE OTHER. THE DIRECTION THAT FEELS SMOOTH IS KNOWN AS THE NAP. FOR A CONSISTENT APPEARANCE, PLAN TO CUT THE FABRIC PIECES FOR EACH CHAIR WITH THE NAP RUNNING DOWN ON THE CHAIR BACK AND FORWARD ON THE SEAT CUSHION.

12 Trim the excess fabric across the corner.

13 On one of the adjoining edges, fold the fabric over the corner fabric; staple it to the plywood.

14 Fold the fabric on the adjoining edge over the corner fabric; staple it to the plywood to complete the corner.

15 Repeat on the remaining corners to finish the seat cushion. Trim the fabric close to the staples.

Covering the Back and Armrests

16 Remove any original foam from the chair back and armrests.

17 Lay the chair back, with its inside surface facing up, on the foam and draw around the edges with the felt-tip marker. Cut out the foam on the lines. Do the same with the armrests, if any.

18 Apply spray adhesive to the inside back. Lay the foam piece on the back and lightly press it in place. Work carefully; the spray adhesive sets up quickly and is not repositionable. Also adhere the foam pieces to the armrests.

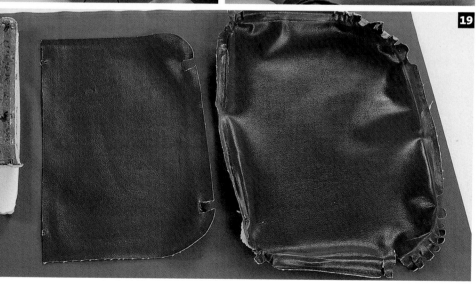

19 Lay the original back coverings and armrests on the right side of the synthetic suede. (For this chair, there was no need to add extra fabric to the inside back or outside back pieces, which were like actual pattern pieces; it *was* necessary to allow extra fabric to wrap around the armrests. Examine your chair's pieces carefully to determine how much extra fabric, if any, to allow when cutting out the pieces.) From left to right in photo 19 are one armrest (shown uncovered with an unattached foam piece underneath), the outside back covering, and the inside back covering.

20 Being careful not to shift the original coverings, cut out the back pieces and armrest pieces from the fabric.

21 On the inside back, apply the spray adhesive to the foam now in place. Center the inside back piece of fabric on the foam, right side up, and smooth the fabric with your hands to make it adhere to the curve.

22 Turn the chair back over. Run a bead of hot glue around the outside edges and wrap the fabric to the back.

23 Make tiny folds in the excess fabric to round the corners.

24 Spray the outside back with adhesive. Center the outside back fabric piece, right side up, and smooth the fabric with your hands to make it adhere to the curve.

25 Center one armrest, with the foam attached, upside down on the wrong side of an armrest fabric piece. Run a bead of hot glue around the inside edges of the armrest. Bring the fabric to the inside, folding in any excess at the curves, and adhere it.

Finishing the Chair

26 Clean the chair frame with trisodium phosphate. Paint with the hammered-metal spray paint, following the manufacturer's instructions.

27 Reassemble the chair.

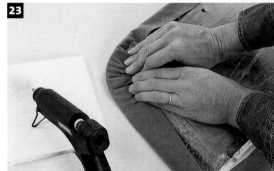

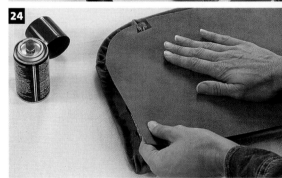

MATERIALS

Steel tape measure

¼-inch graph paper

Blue painter's tape

Paper to protect the countertop

4-inch plain glass tile*

4-inch mosaic glass tile composed of 1-inch pieces*

4-inch white ceramic tile, including bullnose pieces*

¹⁄₁₆-inch tile spacers

Underlayment, available at tile stores and home centers*

12-inch tile cutter, available at tile stores and home centers

Thinset adhesive with a latex additive

Gloves

¼- by ³⁄₈-inch notched trowel

4-inch-square plastic notched adhesive spreader

Tile sponge

Unsanded grout

Grout float

Sanded caulk to match the grout

Tile and grout sealer made for glass tile

MAKEOVER MAGIC

Glass Tile Backsplash

FOR SHEER COLOR IMPACT, nothing can top the look of glass tile. The glass tile in this backsplash includes both plain tiles and prefabricated mosaic tiles. Glass is thinner than standard ceramic tile, making it tricky to apply the two in combination, but the result is a fresh, luminous effect that's well worth the effort. The secret ingredient is a wafflelike underlayment material that brings the glass tile out to the plane of the ceramic tile.

The amount depends on your tile plan. See page 120 for a description of bullnose tiles.

2

TIP

GLASS TILE IS PRICIER THAN

STANDARD CERAMIC TILE,

BUT YOU CAN BUY IT BY THE

SQUARE FOOT RATHER THAN

BY THE BOX, MAKING IT

AFFORDABLE AS AN ACCENT.

YOU MAY BE ABLE TO ORDER A

CUSTOM MIX OF COLORS IN

THE 4-INCH MOSAIC TILES,

AS WAS DONE FOR THIS

BACKSPLASH. THE 4-INCH

PLAIN GLASS TILES WERE

CHOSEN INDIVIDUALLY.

Making a Tile Plan

1 Measure the backsplash area and draw it to scale on graph paper, including outlets and switches. Decide where to begin full tiles. For a backsplash that flanks a sink, it's customary to place full tiles on either side of the sink and work outward, trimming tiles on the ends. It's also customary to place full tiles at counter level and work upward, trimming tiles at the top edge, just below the cabinets. Adjust your plan so that ceramic tiles, not glass tiles, fall where outlets and switches occur.

2 Tape paper to the countertop to protect it. Do a dry-run layout with your tile, including spacers, to check your plan.

Cutting the Underlayment and Jamb Tiles

3 For every glass tile unit consisting of two plain tiles and two mosaic tiles, you'll need a square of underlayment that measures 7 3/4 by 7 3/4 inches (the underlayment is slightly smaller to allow for the spacers). Based on your tile plan, measure and mark the required number of underlayment squares, then cut with scissors.

4 Start tiling at the window jamb (the band of gypsum wallboard surrounding the window). Place a ceramic tile against the jamb, at the bottom, and mark where the top of the tile meets the wall surface, as shown below.

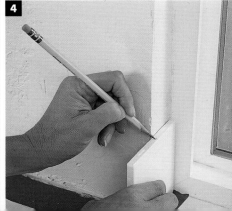

4

5 To cut the tile, place it in the tile cutter so the marked edge is toward you and aligned with the scoring wheel. With the scoring wheel at the back edge of the tile, slide the wheel forward, toward the guide, using even, downward pressure. Score the tile only once. Do not drag the wheel back over the tile.

6 Position the breaker bar on the front edge of the tile. (Make sure the scoring wheel is in its safety well.) Using even, downward pressure, gently squeeze the handle to snap the tile. Mark and cut the remaining jamb tiles.

Setting the Ceramic Tile

7 Mix the thinset according to the manufacturer's instructions. Holding the trowel at an angle, spread the thinset on the jamb and the wall, creating horizontal ridges. Apply the thinset over an area approximately 8 inches high and 24 inches wide (the area covered by two tiles vertically and six tiles horizontally).

8 Set the first jamb tile, with the cut edge toward the window. Set two 1/16-inch spacers, on their sides, under the tile at the counter.

9 Set the second jamb tile above the first, adding a spacer between the two tiles. Set the remaining jamb tiles in the same way.

10 If the bottom backsplash piece nearest the window jamb is a glass tile unit, set a square of underlayment there. Center the underlayment up and down in reference to the first two jamb tiles and slightly to the left (or right, if you're working on the other side of the window) of the jamb tiles, so the edges of the jamb tiles are exposed, as shown.

Bullnose Tiles

Where the edges or corners of the backsplash are exposed, such as at the end of a run of cabinets, you'll need tile with finished edges, known as surface bullnose and radius bullnose tile. Surface bullnose tile features one rounded edge; radius bullnose tile is rounded on two adjacent edges and at the corner.

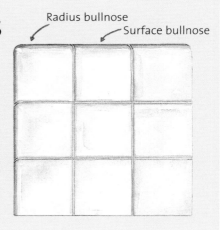

Radius bullnose

Surface bullnose

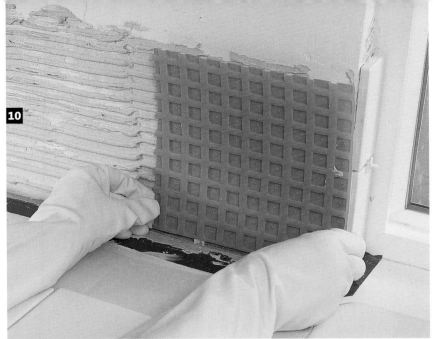

10

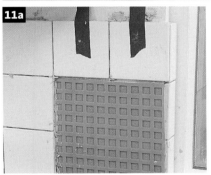

11a

12 Working outward, set the remaining ceramic tiles and underlayment squares according to your tile plan, trimming tile as needed for the upper and side edges. Be sure to use bullnose tiles to complete the exposed edges and corners. (Hidden edges, like those under cabinets, don't require bullnose pieces.)

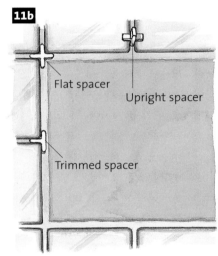

11b

Flat spacer

Upright spacer

Trimmed spacer

11 Set the ceramic tiles surrounding the first underlayment square. Use painter's tape to keep the tiles above the underlayment from slipping. Where three tiles converge at a corner of the underlayment, insert a spacer so it's flat, as you normally would, between the tiles and underlayment. On the sides, you'll need to handle the spacers differently so they won't interfere with the underlayment: either insert the spacer upright between the tiles, or trim a spacer to make a T and set the stem of the T flat between the tiles. See the illustration above right.

12

Setting the Glass Tile

13 Using the 4-inch-square plastic adhesive spreader, apply thinset to the underlayment squares.

14 Set the mosaic and plain tiles in alternating patterns. To copy this four-tile block, set the first mosaic tile in the upper-left area, striving to keep it on the same plane as the ceramic tiles above and to the left. If necessary, remove the mosaic tile and add more thinset.

15 Use strips of blue painter's tape to stabilize the mosaic tile, anchoring it to the ceramic tile on the upper and left edges.

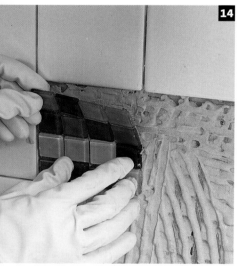

16 Set a plain tile below the mosaic tile and add strips of tape to the side to stabilize the tile. You may need to remove the T spacers at this point and insert whole spacers, or turn the upright spacers down, between the tiles, to further prevent slippage.

17 Set the upper-right plain tile and the lower-right mosaic tile, adding a spacer in the middle of the unit and adjusting the spacers on the edges as needed. Use strips of tape to stabilize the tiles.

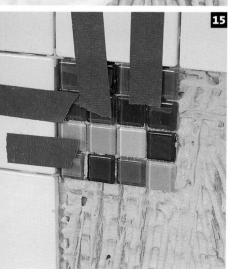

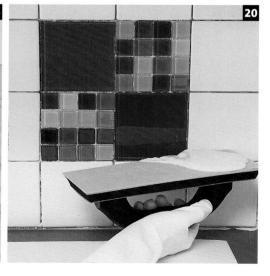

18 Set the remaining glass tiles over the underlayment squares in the same manner. Remove any spacers that are standing up; leave the flat ones embedded in the thinset. Using a damp tile sponge, wipe off any excess thinset on the surface of the tile. Allow the thinset to dry for 24 hours.

Grouting the Tile

19 Mix the grout according to the manufacturer's instructions. (Be sure to wear gloves when you work with grout because it is alkaline and will irritate your skin.)

20 Load the float with grout.

21 Holding the float at a slight angle, as shown, push the grout between the tiles, working in all directions and packing the grout as firmly as possible until it is flush with the top of the tiles.

22 As soon as a haze starts to form, sponge the tile with a wrung-out, nearly dry tile sponge. (A wet sponge will weaken the grout.) Keep a bucket of fresh water handy to rinse the sponge often.

23 Allow the grout to dry overnight.

24 Where the tile meets the counter, run a bead of sanded caulk to strengthen and seal the joint.

25 Seal the tile with the tile and grout sealer.

Pattern
Play

Squares on Point

FACING PAGE: **This contemporary quilt, done in a historic pattern known as Double Four-Patch, plays off the shapes and colors in the vinyl tile floor (see page 108) and the glass tile backsplash (page 118).**

Cookbook Shelf

ABOVE: **Removing two small doors breaks up a run of cabinets above the cooktop and allows easy access to cookbooks. Paint and molding disguise the vent on the original hood, now long gone.**

Up-to-the-Minute Clock

ABOVE: **One-inch glass tiles left over from the backsplash (see page 118) and resin beads embellish a plain plastic clock and make it fun to check the time. Beading glue holds the pieces in place.**

Color-block Valance

BELOW: **Reminiscent of oilcloth, a staple of the 1950s kitchen, this valance "material" consists of raw-edge fabric squares sandwiched and stitched between two sheets of clear craft plastic. Colorful bulldog clips from a stationery store attach to the upper edge and hang from a wire rod.**

125

Utensil Rack

BELOW: An inexpensive rack made from wiggle molding adds a small burst of color to the white tile backsplash and keeps accessories close at hand.

Open Storage

ABOVE: Removing another door turned a storage cabinet under the stove into a display space for a whitewashed woven basket that holds linens; other items hide behind.

Cabinet Face-lift

LEFT: Light dances across the surface of cross-reeded glass in these new cabinet doors. (Refacing existing cabinets is the number-one decorative change in kitchens.) Grasshopper green paint on the inside backs matches the walls.

Confetti Table
Trimmings from the valance decorate the tabletop, a 36-inch square of ¾-inch MDF edged in plain molding and painted pale yellow. A glass top holds the fabric pieces in place and offers other opportunities for display. A chrome pedestal keeps to the retro theme.

Industrial Class

MATERIALS COMMONLY ASSOCIATED with industry—steel, concrete, acrylic, and glass—look warm and appealing in combination with natural elements in this transformed kitchen. Metal panels disguise dated cabinet doors yet leave enough wood showing to soften the hard edges. Concrete troweled over tile says "handcrafted" rather than "man-made." Both surfaces blend with the muted walls for a space-enhancing effect, while the glass-topped table, acrylic chandelier, and utility cart with cutting-board surface stand out in stark contrast. Varied in materials but unified in tone, it all adds up to a harmonious whole.

A kitchen with dark-grouted tile, bright yellow walls, and standard oak cabinets was ripe for renewal; its layout invited a central island or cart.

128

MATERIALS

26-gauge galvanized steel, cut to the required panel sizes (see Step 1), plus scrap (see Step 6)

Fan and outdoor extension cord

Plastic drop cloth

Respirator

Heavy-duty rubber or latex gloves

Muriatic acid, available at home centers and hardware stores (read the label warning carefully)

Disposable paint tray

Natural (sea) sponge

Clear acrylic spray, matte finish

Plywood scraps

Electric drill with $^3/_{16}$- and $^1/_{16}$-inch drill bits

Contact cement

Small paint roller with foam roller covers

Waxed paper

$1^1/_4$-inch #8 flathead screws, four per panel

#8 nickel-plated washers, four per panel

Black spray paint

Wrought-iron handles with bolts (see Step 14)

Heavy paper

MAKEOVER MAGIC

Metal-faced Cabinets

GALVANIZED STEEL PANELS TRANSFORM these traditional oak cabinets, adding bold architectural interest to the kitchen and dramatically changing its color. "Washing" the panels with muriatic acid gives them intriguing visual texture. You can have the panels cut to size by a sheet-metal supplier; have a welder make the wrought-iron handles with holes "tapped" into the ends so they can be bolted to the doors and drawers.

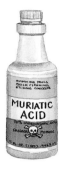

TIP

IF YOU DON'T LIKE THE
EFFECT OF THE FIRST ACID
WASH, YOU CAN REPEAT THE
PROCESS A SECOND, AND
EVEN A THIRD, TIME. IF YOU
STILL DON'T LIKE THE LOOK,
FLIP THE PANELS OVER AND
ACID-WASH THE OTHER
SIDE. LEAVING THE MURIATIC
ACID ON LONGER WON'T
AFFECT THE APPEARANCE
OF THE METAL, HOWEVER;
THE CHEMICAL REACTION
OCCURS IMMEDIATELY,
THEN STOPS.

Cutting the Metal Panels

1 Decide how much of the cabinet doors and drawers you want to cover. (For these doors, the metal panels were sized to cover the raised, cathedral-style frames.) Make a "cabinet map" of your kitchen, noting the location and dimensions of the cabinets and drawers, along with the sizes of their panels. Give your map to the sheet-metal supplier when you have the panels cut. Ask to have the panels cut from sheets that look similar. Also ask to have the razor-sharp edges of the panels and the scrap smoothed for safety.

Acid-washing the Metal Panels

2 Take the following precautions when using muriatic acid: Work outdoors near a faucet and set up a fan to blow the fumes away from you. Protect the work surface with a plastic drop cloth. Wear a respirator and heavy-duty rubber or latex gloves.

3 Pour a small amount of the muriatic acid into the disposable paint tray. Using the sponge, rub the muriatic acid on the first metal panel using a light scrubbing motion. Work quickly for an even effect.

4 Allow the acid to remain on the metal for a few seconds, then wash it off using a spray nozzle attached

to a hose. Towel-dry the panel. Repeat on the other metal panels. When finished, dispose of the excess acid and the sponge and tray as directed on the acid label.

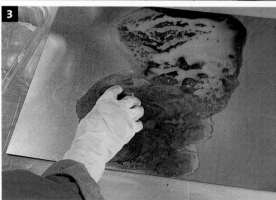

8 Put on the respirator. Lay a panel, wrong side up, next to its door. Mix a small amount of contact cement on a disposable plastic plate. Using the small paint roller with foam cover, roll a thin coat of contact cement on the wrong side of the panel along the edges. Also roll cement on the outside edges of the door panel.

9 To position the panel before cementing it in place, tear off a piece of waxed paper larger than the door to serve as a "slip sheet." Tape two pieces together, if necessary, using blue painter's tape. Lay the waxed paper on the door, covering all but one corner. Place the metal panel on the door, cemented side down, starting at the uncovered corner and lowering the panel onto the waxed paper.

10 Slide the slip sheet out from under the metal panel. Work carefully but quickly; contact cement is not repositionable after just a few seconds. Discard the waxed paper. Glue the rest of the panels. Allow the glue to dry.

11 Using the 1/16-inch drill bit, drill a pilot hole through one hole in a panel and into the wood. Repeat on the remaining corners. Predrill the other doors and drawers in the same way.

5 Spray each panel on the right side with the clear acrylic spray.

Making and Using a Template

6 Determine where to drill the screw holes to attach the panels. For this project, the holes were drilled at the corners, 5/8 inch from each edge, but your doors may require a different placement. To make a template, measure and mark the hole placement on a 90-degree corner of the metal scrap. Place a plywood scrap under the metal scrap and, using the 3/16-inch drill bit, drill through the metal at the mark. Using the template, drill through each corner of each panel.

Gluing the Panels

7 Remove the drawer pulls and cabinet handles, if any. Remove the cabinet doors and drawer fronts; mark their location on the back. Pair each panel with its corresponding door or drawer.

132

Attaching the Panels

12 Screw the flathead screws into a scrap of plywood; lay the washers on the plywood so they do not touch. Spray the screws and washers with black spray paint.

13 Attach the metal panels to the doors using the painted screws and washers. Touch up the hardware, if necessary, with black paint and a cotton swab.

Attaching the Handles and Remounting the Cabinets

14 Have the welder make handles to fit the width of the metal panels and tap holes in each end to accommodate bolts. The handles on these doors and drawers were made from 5/16-inch-diameter wrought iron; they are 1/2 inch narrower than the metal panels and accommodate 1 1/2-inch #10 roundhead bolts. Vertical placement on the doors is a matter of choice, but avoid the hinges; these handles are positioned 3 inches from the lower or upper edges. The handles on the drawers are centered.

15 Using heavy paper, make a template the width of a metal panel. The height of the template should equal the vertical placement of the handle plus several inches. Draw a horizontal line at the desired height of the handle. Position the

template on a panel; anchor it with blue painter's tape. Center the handle on the line. Draw a circle around each handle end and mark the middle of each circle.

16 Using the 1/16-inch drill bit, drill pilot holes through the template and metal panel and into the wood. Using the 3/16-inch drill bit, drill the holes through the wood for the bolts.

17 Position the handle over the drilled holes. Screw the bolts into the handle from the back.

18 Repeat Steps 15 through 17 to attach handles to the remaining doors and drawers.

19 Rehang the doors. Reinstall the drawer fronts and slide the drawers back in place.

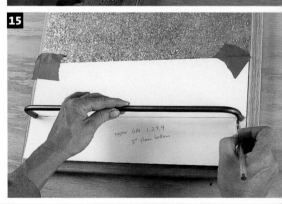

Blue painter's tape

Plastic sheets

Kraft paper

Large fan

Eye and ear protection

Respirator

Heavy-duty leather or
synthetic gloves

Right-angle grinder

1-pound coffee can

Portland cement, gray
and white

90-mesh sand

Concrete polymer

One 1-gallon bucket and
two 5-gallon buckets

Electric drill with mixing
paddle bit

2½- by 12-inch cement
finishing trowel

Heavy-duty rubber or
latex gloves

Spray bottle with
fine-mist nozzle

220-grit sandpaper

"Sandstone"
concentrated concrete
stain

2-inch paintbrush

Tile sponge

Water-based sealer

MAKEOVER MAGIC

Concrete Counter

CONVENTIONAL WISDOM dictates that old tile be removed before a new surface is installed, but this project covers it with the new material, concrete enhanced by a polymer that makes the surface as durable as it is striking. Cement and sand—the dry ingredients—are inexpensive, but typical bags contain much more than you'll need; look for a concrete supplier who will sell you small quantities. When the surface begins to wear, apply another coat of the water-based sealer.

Preparing the Surface

1 Remove the switch plates and outlet covers on the backsplash; cover the openings with blue painter's tape. Protect the cabinets with plastic sheets and the floor with kraft paper.

2 Open all the windows and doors and place the fan in a position where it will push the air through the room and outdoors. Put on the eye protection, ear protection, respirator, and heavy-duty gloves. Holding the grinder at a 30-degree angle, rough up the surface of the tile so it will accept the wet concrete. It's not necessary to grind every square inch.

3 Use the claw end of a hammer to rough up the corners or other spots you can't reach with the grinder.

Mixing the Concrete

Each batch of concrete will cover approximately 65 square feet; you'll need two or three batches.

4 You'll use the 1-pound coffee can for measuring the concrete ingredients. Premix 2 cans of white

cement and 1/6 can of gray cement in the 1-gallon bucket. Stir the mixture to blend thoroughly.

5 Combine 2 cans of the premixed cement from the previous step (discard the leftover) and 2 cans of 90-mesh sand in a 5-gallon bucket and stir the mixture to blend thoroughly.

6 Combine 1 can of concrete polymer and 1 can of water in the other 5-gallon bucket. Add the dry ingredients to the liquid and mix for several minutes using the electric drill with mixing paddle bit until the consistency is smooth.

Troweling the Backsplash and Deck

7 Using the cement finishing trowel and wearing heavy-duty rubber or latex gloves, spread the concrete over the tile backsplash. Work in 2- to 3-foot sections, trailing off the edges to avoid buildup where you stop and start. If the concrete is too thin and won't adhere to the backsplash, let the mixture rest in the bucket for a few minutes

TIP GRINDING THE TILE PRODUCES A LOT OF DUST AND A STRONG ODOR. WEARING A RESPIRATOR IS A MUST. TAKE FREQUENT BREAKS OUTDOORS.

8

9

10

13

until it sets up a little. The concrete has an "open" (workable) time of approximately 15 minutes. If the mixture seems too thick at any time during its application, spray the concrete on the backsplash with a fine mist of water from the spray bottle. Make the surface as smooth as possible, but don't attempt to cover the tile or fill the grout lines completely with the first application; this is merely a base coat.

8 Trowel a base coat of concrete onto the "deck" (countertop).

Troweling the Edge

9 To apply the concrete to the edge, load the trowel and hold it parallel to the countertop, just below the lower edge of the tile trim, as shown.

10 Roll the trowel up and over the edge, coating the trim surface evenly. If your trim has a square edge, hold the trowel at an angle against the trim and drag the trowel upward without rolling it over the edge.

11 The temperature and humidity will affect the drying time. Err on the side of safety and let the concrete dry overnight.

12 Allow any leftover concrete to set up in the bucket until it's firm enough to hold together. Turn the

bucket upside down to release the concrete, and break it apart to make it easier to dispose of.

Troweling Additional Coats

13 Once the first coat is dry, sand down rough spots using the 220-grit sandpaper. Spray the surface with a fine mist of water to help the second coat adhere to the base coat.

14 Mix a second batch of concrete. Trowel a second coat onto the backsplash as you did the first, striving to cover the surface more completely this time.

15 Trowel a second coat onto the deck.

16 Trowel a second coat over the edge. To round the edge, use part of a plastic milk jug or a coffee can lid, bending and pulling it toward you as shown. The polymer makes the mixture sticky, like white glue. If it

14

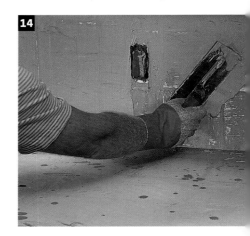

seems too sticky and the plastic isn't gliding smoothly, spray the concrete with just enough water to give the surface a sheen and continue working. If the concrete is too wet, allow it to dry a little before continuing.

17 Allow the second coat to dry; sand if needed. Apply a third coat to the backsplash, deck, and edge if needed. Allow to dry; sand.

Staining the Surface

18 Mix the concentrated concrete stain in a ratio of 1 part stain to 10 parts water in a glass bowl not used for food. Don't be alarmed that the color of the stain is not what you expect: the mineral salts in the stain, which is acidic, react chemically with the cement to bring up the color.

19 Cover the deck with plastic and place a bucket of fresh water nearby; put on the rubber or latex gloves. With just a little bit of stain

on your paintbrush, apply it to the backsplash in a circular motion. Remove the plastic and apply the stain to the deck, followed by the trim. Be sure not to drip on the surface—drips can't be wiped up and will leave prominent, permanent marks. Have a helper work alongside you to wipe off excess stain with a tile sponge, rinsing the sponge often.

20 After 48 hours, wipe down the surface with a damp sponge to remove any stain residue.

Sealing the Surface

21 Following the manufacturer's instructions, seal the backsplash and deck with the water-based sealer.

TIP

EXPERIMENT WITH DRIED CONCRETE ON A SCRAP OF HARDBOARD TO FIND THE RATIO OF STAIN TO WATER THAT YOU LIKE. ADD MORE WATER, AND THE SURFACE WILL HAVE A SUBTLE PATINA. USE LESS, AND THE COLOR WILL BE MORE INTENSE.

MATERIALS

Metal cart on casters

Black spray paint

Electric drill with
³/₁₆-inch drill bit and
combination counter-
sink–pilot hole bit

Nine ³/₁₆-inch U-bolts,
each 4 inches long,
with eighteen nuts

Twenty-two 1½- by
1½-inch pieces of
figured maple, each
40 inches long

Ten ¼- by 1½-inch
pieces of English walnut,
each 40 inches long

Carpenter's square

Router

Slot cutter for 0mm
biscuits (or a plate joiner)

C-clamps

Fifty-one 0mm biscuits

FDA-approved wood
glue for cutting boards

Glue roller

Pony (pipe) clamps

Circular saw

"Maple" wood filler

80-, 120-, and 220-grit
sandpaper

Roundover bit

Eight 2-inch #8 screws

Heavy mineral oil

WOOD SHOP

Cutting-board Cart

YOU CAN DUPLICATE the look of an expensive kitchen cart with this simple
woodworking project. The cart itself came from a discount hardware store;
the maple and walnut pieces that make up the cutting board were cut by a
cabinet shop. For a different-size cart, add 3½ inches to the cart length for
the cut length of the wood pieces. Add or subtract pieces, or trim the outer
pieces, to make the cutting board 1 inch wider than the cart.

FINISHED SIZE wood top: 37½ by 25 inches; metal cart: 36½ inches long,
24 inches wide, 32 inches tall

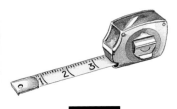

Preparing the Cart

1 Cover the casters on the cart, shown unpainted at right. Working outdoors, spray the cart with the black spray paint.

2 Using the electric drill and ³/₁₆-inch bit, drill three equidistant holes on each long edge and down the center of the upper tray for the U-bolts.

Marking the Pieces

3 Select eighteen maple pieces for the cutting board; set aside the remaining four pieces for the support frame.

4 Arrange the maple and walnut pieces as shown below. The maple pieces were paired in the central area; single pieces were placed at the edges.

4

Single maple strip

Paired maple strips

Walnut strips

5

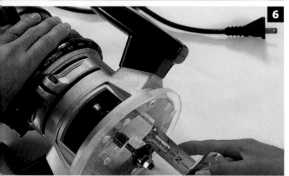

6

7

16 inches from the second line for the slots near the other end. (This side of the pieces will become the B side of the board.) Repeat to mark groups of the remaining strips.

Cutting the Slots

6 On the router, set the slot cutter depth to ⅝ inch as shown. (Or use a plate joiner.)

7 Clamp the outside maple piece to your work surface, using paper or fabric scraps to protect the wood. Position another piece of maple to support the router. (It's essential to keep the router parallel to the piece being cut, not tilted.) Cut three slots for biscuits on the inside edge, centering them on the marked lines. Cut slots for biscuits on both edges of the remaining pieces except for the other outside strip, which is cut only on the inside edge. Where a

strip of walnut is sandwiched between maple pieces, clamp the walnut strip to one maple piece and cut them as one strip. Check the fit of the biscuits as you go.

Joining the Pieces

8 Working with a section of the cutting board consisting of three or four maple pieces and the companion walnut pieces, roll glue sparingly onto the slotted edges of the strips and drip a little glue into the slots. Insert the biscuits. Work efficiently; wood glue sets up quickly.

9 Clamp the pieces together with the pony clamps, applying even pressure. Use dry (not damp or wet) paper towels to wipe off the excess glue. Allow the glue to dry as specified in the manufacturer's instructions.

5 Group a section of four maple pieces and any companion walnut strips. Approximately 4 inches from the ends, mark a line perpendicular to the lengthwise edges using the carpenter's square. This line is for cutting the first slots for the biscuits (the oval-shaped wafers of compressed wood that join the maple and walnut pieces). Keeping the wood pieces together, measure and mark a second line 16 inches from the first line for the center slots, and another line

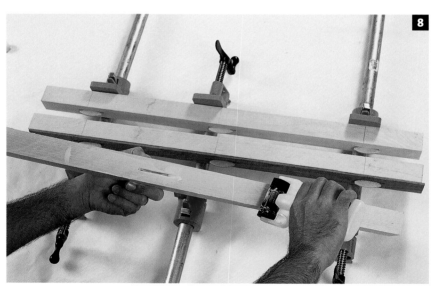

8

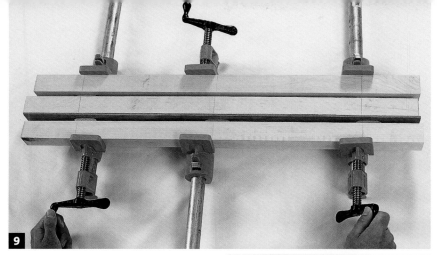

10 Repeat Steps 8 and 9 with the remaining sections of maple and walnut pieces. Glue the sections together; clamp.

Finishing the Board

11 Measure and mark the board to 37½ inches (or your finished length, if it is different). Trim the ends with the circular saw.

12 Fill any imperfections or nicks on the A side of the board with the maple-colored wood filler; allow to dry.

13 Sand the A side of the board, starting with the 80-grit sandpaper, followed by the 120- and 220-grit sandpaper.

14 Using your router with the roundover bit, finish the edges.

Attaching the Support Frame

15 Measure the length and width of the cart tray's interior. If there are obstacles, such as screws protruding through the sides, take the measurements *inside* these obstacles so the support frame will

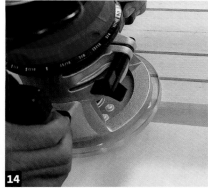

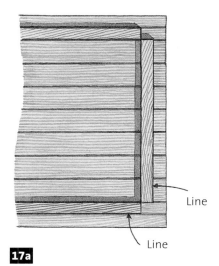

Line

Line

sit inside them. Draw a rectangle to these measurements on the B side of the board, carefully positioning it so the board will overhang the cart by the same distance on all four sides.

16 To make the support frame, cut the four remaining maple pieces to the lengths of the drawn lines, less 3 inches.

17 Position the support pieces so their outside edges are on the drawn lines. Using the #8 screws and the combination countersink–pilot hole bit, screw the support pieces to the board.

Finishing the Cart

18 Apply heavy mineral oil to the A side of the board using a clean rag.

19 To attach the U-bolts, thread a nut onto a bolt. Insert the bolt through the cart tray from the underside; thread another nut onto the bolt and tighten. Repeat for each bolt.

20 Set the board into the tray.

Special Effects

Rough-hewn Table

Impressive in scale, a table made of incense cedar 4 by 4s and 2 by 4s has the visual presence to fill—but not crowd—the dining area. The lumber was colored using a mixture of black walnut stain and linseed oil. Black glass repeats the black bolts and corner brackets that hold it all together and reiterates the color of the appliances.

Pot Rack

BELOW: **A welding shop fabricated this inexpensive iron pot rack, which does double duty as a nontraditional window treatment. The hooks are available through kitchenware sources.**

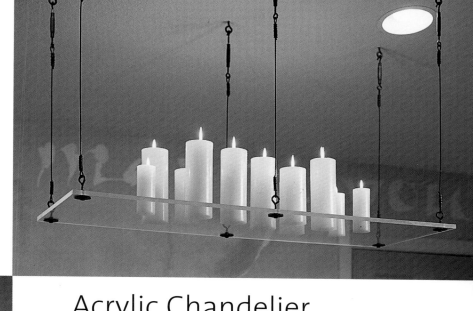

Acrylic Chandelier

ABOVE: **Unlikely materials—acrylic plastic and airline cable—combine to create an atmosphere of austere elegance in the dining area. The chandelier hangs from turnbuckles attached to eye screws.**

Open Shelving

BELOW: **Cabinets need not all look the same in a kitchen, as these open shelves illustrate. Painting the backs the same low-intensity green as the walls provides a visual break from the metal-faced doors and expands the sense of space.**

Index

Numbers in **boldface** refer to additional photographs.

A handpainted cotton-linen table runner with grommets on the ends dresses the table in simple style. See "Sea Change," page 84.